GCSE English
for WJEC

Ken Elliott

Ted Snell

Barry Childs

Don Astley

From Harcourt

Heinemann Educational Publishers
Halley Court, Jordan Hill, Oxford OX2 8EJ
Part of Harcourt Education

Heinemann is the registered trademark of Harcourt Education Limited

© Don Astley, Barry Childs, Ken Elliott, Ted Snell 2007

First published 2007

12 11 10 09 08 07
10 9 8 7 6 5 4 3 2 1

British Library Cataloguing in Publication Data is available from the British Library on request.

ISBN: 978 0 435368 04 3

Designed by Wooden Ark Studio
Typeset and illustrated by 🐟 Tek-Art, Croydon, Surrey
Original illustrations © Harcourt Education Limited 2007
Picture research by Zooid Pictures Limited
Cover design by Wooden Ark Studio
Cover photo: © Getty images
Printed by CPI Bath Press

Acknowledgements
The authors and publisher would like to thank the following individuals and organisations for permission to reproduce photographs:
Felipe Rodriguez/Alamy pp2/113; Stone/Getty Images p9; Getty images/Stone p11; Tim Wright/Corbis p13; Richard T. Nowitz/Corbis p15; Corbis p20; Helene Rogers/Alamy p23; Emma Rian/zefa/Corbis p24; Corbis UK Ltd p27; kolvenbach/Alamy p30; Getty Images/PhotoDisc /OS28003 p32; Corbis UK Ltd p34; Harald Sund/Riser/Getty Images p38; Morgan David de Lossy/Corbis UK Ltd p42; Getty Images/ First Light pp46/49; John Conrad/Corbis UK Ltd p53; National Geographic/Getty Images pp54–55; Helen Atkinson/Reuters/Corbis UK Ltd pp56/91; David Cumming/Eye Ubiquitous/Corbis UK Ltd p58; Jeff Morgan/Alamy p62; Becky Luigart-Stayner/Corbis UK Ltd p64; Microzoa/Stone/Getty Images p68; Peter Worth/ Alamy p69; Peter Oliver/Alamy p70 (top); David Lyons/Alamy p70 (middle); David Jackson/Alamy p70 (bottom); Steve Prezant/Corbis UK Ltd p74; Kevin White/Alamy pp75/81; Getty Images/Imagebank p77; John James/Alamy p84; Terry W. Eggers/Corbis UK Ltd p86; K. Koczera/plainpicture/ Alamy p89; Reuters/Corbis p93; Hulton-Deutsch Collection/Corbis p94; Bruno De Hogues/Sygma/Corbis UK Ltd p99; Getty Images/PhotoDisc p101; Kirstie Tweed/Veer/Corbis p102; plainpicture GmbH & Co. KG/Alamy p103; Dbimages/Alamy p107; M.Thomsen/Zefa/Corbis p114; M.Thomsen/Zefa/Corbis p120; Getty Images/PhotoDisc /61066 p121; Corbis UK Ltd p127; Andy Bishop/Alamy p128; Maurice van der Velden/ iStockphoto p135; Paul Thompson/Corbis UK Ltd p137; The Image Bank/Getty p139; National Express Ltd p142; Floyd Anderson/iStockphoto p143; Getty Images/ National Geographic p148; Magnus Rew/Dorling Kindersley/DK Images p149; Mark A. Johnson/Alamy p151; Lew Robertson/ Corbis UK Ltd p153; Getty Images/PhotoDisc /18299 p154; Design Pics Inc./Alamy p156; Gone Wild Limited/Photonica/Getty Images p160; Mike Bentley/iStockphoto p161; Corbis UK Ltd p164; C.W. Disney/Everett/Rex Features p166; PhotoDisc. PhotoLink. S. Meltzer p171; Martin Jenkinson/ Alamy p173; Rex Features/Peter Brooker p174.

Every effort has been made to contact copyright holders of material reproduced in this book. Any omissions will be rectified in subsequent printings if notice is given to the publishers.
Extract slightly adapted from 'Almost Human' by Ruth Rendell, from *Collected Stories* by Ruth Rendell, published by Hutchinson. Copyright © Ruth Rendell. Reprinted with permission of PFD on behalf of Ruth Rendell; Extract from *On Beulah Height* by Reginald Hill, published by HarperCollins. Reprinted with permission of A P Watt Limited and HarperCollins Publishers Limited; Extract from *Farenheit 451* by Ray Bradbury. Reprinted with the permission of Don Congdon Associates, Inc., Copyright 1953, renewed 1981 by Ray Bradbury. Extract from *Gorilla My Love* by Toni Cade Bambara, published by The Women's Press. Reprinted with kind permission of the Womens Press; Extract from *City of the Mind* by Penelope Lively, published by Penguin Books. Reprinted with permission of David Higham Associates Limited; Extract adapted from 'Customers' by Penelope Lively, from *A Pack of Cards* published by Penguin Books. Copyright © Penelope Lively. Reprinted with permission of David Higham Associates Limited; Extract from *Ginger You're Barmy* by David Lodge, Published by Secker & Warburg. Reprinted with permission of The Random House Group Limited; Extract from *Changing Babies* By Deborah Moggach, published by William Heinemann. Copyright © Deborah Moggach. Permission granted by Curtis Brown Group Limited; Extract slightly adapted from *A Child in Time* by Ian McEwan, published by Jonathan Cape. Reprinted with permission of The Random House Group Limited; Extracts from 'Broken Homes' from *Lover of their Time* by William Trevor. Copyright © William Trevor. Reprinted by permission of PFD on behalf of William Trevor; Extract from *The Ghost Road* by Pat Barker (Viking 1995, Penguin Books 1996) Copyright © Pat Barker 1995. Reprinted with permission of Penguin Books UK; Extracts 'The Whirlpool Rapids – two stories about Emma' from *Bluebeard's Egg* by Margaret Attwood, published by Jonathan Cape. Reprinted with permission of The Random House Group Limited; Extract from *Mother Can You Help Me?* by Margaret Forster. Copyright © Margaret Forster. Reprinted with permission of the Sayle Agency and the author; 'The sunshine isle where teenage tearaways are sent to learn a lesson' by Lucie Morris, *Daily Mail*. Reprinted with permission of Solo Syndications; Article regarding Spencer Oliver by Niall Hickman, *Daily Mail*, 1998. Reprinted with permission of Solo Syndications; 'Recycling can be a complete waste (of time)' by Robin Yapp, *Daily Mail*, December 31st 2003. Reprinted with permission of Solo Syndications; Extract from 'Going the distance' by Anne Johnson, published in *The Guardian*, 6th April, 2004. Copyright © Anne Johnson. Reprinted with kind permission of the author; Text from Llandudno leaflet. Copyright © Conwy County Borough Council. www.visitllandudno.org.uk. Reprinted with kind permission; Extract from an old article 'Boiling the Frog' from the Top Gear website; Use of headline 'A Bit of Rootail Therapy' by Allison Martin, *The Mirror*, 13th October, 2006. Reprinted with permission; Use of headline 'We're all going bananas' by Robin McKie, *The Observer*, June 2002. © Guardian News & Media Ltd. Reprinted with permission; Use of headline 'Rubbish attitudes laying waste to our landscapes' by John Ingham, *Express*, 8th May, 2002. Reprinted with permission; 'I'm In' advertisement is reproduced with permission of Oxfam GB, Oxfam House, John Smith Drive, Cowley, Oxford OX4 2JY, UK www.oxfam.org.uk. Oxfam GB does not necessarily endorse any text or activities that accompany the materials; Fairtrade Banana Campaign sheet. Copyright © Fairtrade Foundation. Reprinted with kind permission; Use of page from Big Pit leaflet. Reprinted with kind permission; British Gas Logo reprinted with permission; Lloyds TSB logo reprinted with permission; Playstation logo. Reprinted with permission of Sony Computer Entertainment Europe; Penguin logo. Reprinted with permission; The Oxfam logo is reproduced with permission of Oxfam GB, Oxfam House, John Smith Drive, Cowley, Oxford OX4 2JY, UK www.oxfam.org.uk Oxfam GB does not necessarily endorse any text or activities that accompany the materials; Extract from *Chance Witness* by Matthew Parris (Penguin Books 2002) Copyright © Matthew Parris 2002. Reprinted with permission of Penguin Books UK; Extract from *The Road to Wigan Pier* by George Orwell. Copyright © George Orwell, 1937, by permission of Bill Hamilton as the Literary Executor of the Estate of the Late Sonia Brownell Orwell and Secker & Warburg Ltd. Reprinted by permission of A. M. Heath; Extract of text only from 'Sun Facts: The Burning Issues'. Reprinted with the kind permission of Health Promotion, Milton Keynes Primary Care Trust; Book review of 'The Lighthouse' by P D James, review by Christina Konig, *The Times*, Saturday, 16th September, 2006. Reprinted with permission of NI Syndications; Film review slightly adapted 'The Devil and Daniel Johnston' by Robert Hanks, *The Independent*, Friday 5th May, 2006. Used with permission; Extract from *Man and Boy* by Tony Parsons published by HarperCollins. Copyright © Tony Parsons. Reprinted with permission of HarperCollins Publishers Limited; Extracts from Friends of the Earth leaflet. © Friends of the Earth. Reprinted with permission.

Contents

Introduction

How will this book help me?

The aim of this book is to prepare you for the two GCSE English exams that you will be taking. The book is written by the most senior examiners at WJEC who have many years' experience of writing and marking the English exam papers. So, you are getting:

- the inside view of what is expected of you
- advice throughout the book on how to improve your reading and writing responses.

You will also find examples of successful and not so successful exam answers to help improve your responses. Activities are provided to help you to learn, practise and improve the skills you will need to succeed.

There are also examples of complete exam papers, written specifically for this student book, to help test your learning.

This book will take you through the types of questions that you will face in the two English exams, using real exam materials. You should then not only know how to improve your answers, but also feel confident as you go into the exams. Overall, the examiners who wrote this book are aiming to help you take control of your learning.

What is in the GCSE English exams?

Whether you are taking Foundation or Higher tier, there are two exam papers in GCSE English. These are as follows:

Paper 1

How long is the exam?	2 hours.
What is in the exam?	Section A is a test of Reading.
	Section B is a test of Writing.
What is in Section A?	There is a short story or extract from a novel of about one-and-a-half sides in length followed by four questions each carrying ten marks. On the Foundation tier, occasionally, there will be two questions worth five marks and three worth ten marks each.
How much should I write?	Depending on the size of your handwriting, aim to write between two-thirds and a side for each answer in Section A.
How long should I spend on Section A?	About 55 minutes.
What is in Section B?	You will be asked to produce two pieces of writing. Each is worth 20 marks.
What is the first task?	The first task requires you to inform/explain/describe – with the emphasis on the last of these. For example: 'Describe the scene at a market.'
How much should I write?	Depending on the size of your handwriting, aim to write about one side.
What is the second task in Section B?	From five choices, you are required to write to explore/imagine/entertain – for example, tell a story or write an autobiographical account.
How much should I write?	Depending on the size of your handwriting, aim to write around two sides.
How long should I spend on Section B?	About 65 minutes: 25 minutes on the first task and 40 minutes on the second task.

Paper 2

How long is the exam?   2 hours.

What is in the exam?   Section A is a test of Reading.

Section B is a test of Writing.

What is in Section A?   There are two passages to read – one a media text and the other non-fiction. There will be four questions on the texts each carrying ten marks. One of the questions will ask you to compare the texts in some way. On the Foundation tier, occasionally, there will be two questions worth five marks and three worth ten marks each.

How much should I write?   Depending on the size of your handwriting, aim to write about half to one side for each answer in Section A.

How long should I spend on Section A?   About 50 minutes (no more than 1 hour).

What is in Section B?   You will be asked to produce two pieces of writing. Each is worth 20 marks. The order of the two tasks might vary.

What are the tasks?   One task will require you to argue/persuade/advise – for example, write a letter.

The other task will require you to analyse/review/comment – for example, write a review.

How much should I write?   Depending on the size of your handwriting, aim to write between one and two sides for each piece of writing.

How long should I spend on Section B?   About 70 minutes, so about 35 minutes on each piece of writing (no less than 30 minutes).

How is this book organised?

This book is divided into five sections.

- Sections 1 to 4 cover the reading and writing parts of the two exams.
- Section 5 provides complete examples of Paper 1 and Paper 2 for you to practise.

As well as providing teaching and advice, this book also includes the following features.

- 'What will I learn?': at the beginning of each mini-section you will find a summary objective box.
- 'Activity': throughout the book you will find the activities, which are easy to find in a distinctive box.
- 'Examiner tip': throughout the book you will find additional tips from the authors to help prepare you for the two exams.
- 'Remember': throughout the book you will find reminders about points of learning and other key tips.
- 'What did the examiner think?': after a sample student response you will often find the comments from the examiner on that answer.
- 'What have I learnt?': at the end of the first four sections you will find a summary box that encourages you to reflect on your learning and identify where you feel confident and where you need to go back to a teaching and learning point.

What additional resources are there?

Your teacher may also have the Teacher's Guide that accompanies this student book. The Teacher's Guide contains:

- answers and guidance
- photocopiable resources for students including blank activity grids
- additional resources including activities, student responses and examiner comments
- a customisable CD-ROM Word version of the Teacher's Guide.

Introduction

What will Section A of Paper 1 look like?

In Section A of Paper 1 you will have to read an unseen passage from a novel or a short story. You will then answer a series of questions designed to test your understanding of what you have read.

Each year the exam includes a different passage, so you cannot predict what will be used. Also, it is unlikely that you will have read it before.

What will the questions be like?

The good news is that the questions are fairly predictable. This section of the exam aims to test your understanding of what you have read, rather than your ability to understand complicated questions. You can prepare yourself by practising the types of question you are likely to be asked. Although there is sometimes a question that asks you to consider the whole passage, most questions refer to specific lines.

You need a reliable technique for dealing with unseen passages. You also need to understand how to approach the different types of question. This is exactly what this book will prepare you for.

The wording of the questions varies and you cannot be certain which questions will appear. However, there are **five** basic types of question in this exam. Examples appear on page 7; if you practise these question types, you should be well prepared to face the exam with confidence.

What should I do?

You have around 55 minutes to complete this section of the paper. Your answers should be of roughly equal length and you should allocate your time very carefully. You will have not more than 10–15 minutes to answer each question, and each answer should be about two-thirds of a side in length.

1. First, you should read the whole passage quickly but carefully. This will take you about six or seven minutes.

> **Examiner tip**
>
> It's a good idea to mark on the exam paper the lines referred to in each question. Writing about other lines won't gain you any marks, and will waste your time.

2. Next, you should look at the first question and read the lines it refers to. The questions will take you through the passage in sections. The last question may ask you to consider the whole passage.

Paper 1 Section A sample question types

Below are examples of the types of question you could be asked in Section A of your Paper 1 exam. Reading these will help you to understand what you are preparing for as you work through this section of the book.

1. Locating and retrieving information
- What clues or details can you find to prove something?
- What evidence can you find to prove something?

2. Personal response
- What are your thoughts and feelings about a character or relationship?
- What impressions do you get of a character, or relationship or place?
- What do you learn about a character or relationship?

3. Character response
- What are the character's thoughts and feelings?
- What is going through the character's mind?
- How does a character react, or behave or change?
- Why does a character act or behave in a certain way?

4. The craft of the writer
- How does the writer convey, create, make or suggest?
- What happens in these lines? How and why do you react to what happens?
- How effective is the ending?
- What are your thoughts and feelings as you read these lines?

5. Empathetic response
- Imagine you are a character.

Locating and retrieving information

What will I learn?

In this unit I will:
- learn the techniques used to locate and retrieve information
- practise answering 'search and find' questions.

'Search and find' questions ask you to locate and retrieve information. They test your ability to spot relevant details or evidence; you do not normally have to do very much with the information you select. Provided you are accurate and thorough in your selection of material from the passage, this should be an opportunity to gain marks quickly and quite easily.

These questions can be asked in two ways.
1. What clues or details can you find to prove or show something?
2. What evidence can you find to prove or show something?

'Clues or details' questions

Below is an example of a 'search and find' question. Read the question and the extract that follows (a description of a man called Richard, who is preparing to kill someone for money). The number in brackets tells you the number of marks available for this question.

What clues are there to suggest that Richard is well organised and experienced as a hired killer? (5)

So he had to kill a man to get it? It wouldn't be the first time. [...]

He put the car in Templewood Avenue as near as he could to the point where the path left it to wind across West Heath. This was to be on the safe side. There weren't any real risks, but it was always as well to ensure a quick getaway. He strolled into the path. It led
5 between the fences of gardens, a steep lane about five feet wide, with steps here and there where the incline grew too sharp. At the summit was a street lamp and another about fifty yards further on where the path became walled. Between the lights was a broader sandy space dotted about with trees and shrubs. He'd do it here, Richard decided. He'd stand among the trees until the man appeared from the walled end, wait until he left

10 the first pool of light but hadn't yet reached the second, and catch him in the darkest part. [...]

Luckily, the bitter cold was keeping most people indoors. As soon as this thought had passed through his mind, he heard footsteps in the distance and his hand tightened on the padded metal bar in his pocket. [...]

15 Footsteps. Yes, it was time. Ten to nine, and evidently he was of a punctual habit. So much the worse for him. Richard kept perfectly still, staring at the dark hole between the walls, until the vague shape of his quarry appeared at the end of the tunnel. As the man came towards the light, he tensed, closing his hand over the bar. Her description had been precise. [...]

20 The man advanced casually and confidently and the dark space received him. Richard stepped out from among the trees, raised his arm and struck. The man gave a grunt, not much louder than a hiccup, and fell heavily.

The question is worth five marks. In this exam, that means you have to find five pieces of evidence to answer the question. You could list them as bullet points, as in Answer 1 below, or write in paragraphs, as in Answer 2.

Answer 1 – any five of the following

- 'It wouldn't be the first time.'
- He parks the car ready for a quick getaway.
- He 'strolled' (this shows he is calm about the whole matter).
- He chooses a dark area for the attack.
- He has a padded metal bar.
- He keeps perfectly still as his victim approaches.
- He only has to strike his victim once.

Examiner tip

Remember, bullet points must still make sense, even though they are brief and to the point.

Answer 2

> The fact that 'it wouldn't be the first time' shows that he is an experienced killer. He parks the car ready for a quick getaway and he stays calm about the whole matter. He chooses a dark area for the attack, and he has a padded metal bar. He keeps perfectly still as his victim approaches. He only has to strike his victim once.

The points made are the same; the only difference is the presentation. Both answers would gain full marks. Examiners will tick each point that deserves a mark, up to a maximum of five.

'Evidence' questions

This is a slightly different way of asking you to locate and retrieve information. Read the extract below, which describes a policeman, then complete Activity 1, which gives you an example of this type of question.

> The eye of God which makes no distinctions of persons was beaming with equal benevolence on Police Constable Hector as he left Mid-Yorkshire police station and began his slow perambulation through the centre of town. His gait was not exactly majestic; in fact he moved as if under the control of a trainee puppeteer who'd got his
> 5   strings tangled. This was an apt metaphor for how his superiors felt. Finding a niche for a man of his talents had been difficult. For a time the conventional wisdom was that the public weal would be best served by keeping Hector hidden in the bowels of the building, 'helping' with records. But the increase in computerisation had put an end to that. Though specifically forbidden to touch anything that had switches, buttons,
> 10 lights or made a humming noise, Hector's mere presence seemed somehow perilous to

the proper function of electronic equipment. 'He's a human virus,' declared the sergeant in charge. 'Get him out of here else he'll be into the Pentagon War Room in a fortnight!' A spell on
15 the desk had brought complaints from the public that they got better service from Mid-Yorks Water. Finally, when the *Evening Post* supported a campaign to get bobbies back on the beat […] the Assistant Chief Constable said, 'Well, we
20 can manage *that* at any rate,' and Hector was returned into the community.

But not without some necessary fail-safes. He had to radio in every thirty minutes, else a car was sent out to look for him. If his assistance was required
25 in any matter more serious than a request for the time, he had to contact Control for instructions. And in particular, he was strictly forbidden to make any attempt to direct traffic, as his last
30 venture in that area had resulted in a gridlock which made the Chief Constable miss a train.

The eye of God	the sun	**gait**	walk
benevolence	kindness	**niche**	role
perambulation	patrol	**Control**	the police station
public weal	the public welfare		

Activity 1

Find and note down at least ten pieces of evidence, either in bullet point form or in paragraphs, to answer the following question.

What evidence can you find to show that Constable Hector is a hopeless policeman? (10)

Remember that the number 10 in brackets tells you how many marks are available for the question. You should therefore include at least ten pieces of evidence for your answer.

How many pieces of evidence did you find? On the following page are examples of answers. Check which pieces of evidence you found and see if you missed any. Remember that in this type of question you can answer using either bullets or paragraphs.

Answer 1 – any ten of the following

- His patrol is described as 'slow'.
- His walk is 'not exactly majestic' (clumsy and awkward).
- He moves as if a 'trainee puppeteer' is controlling him and has got the strings tangled.
- His superiors find it difficult to work out a role for him.
- He is kept hidden in the bowels of the building 'helping' with records.
- He is not allowed to touch anything electronic.
- The sergeant describes him as a 'human virus'.
- The public complain when he is on duty at the station desk.
- He has to radio in every thirty minutes.
- He is not allowed to deal with anything more serious than a request for the time.
- He is definitely not allowed to direct traffic.
- He caused 'gridlock'.
- He made the Chief Constable miss his train.

Answer 2

> His patrol is described as 'slow' and his walk is 'not exactly majestic'. He moves as if a 'trainee puppeteer' is controlling him and has got the strings tangled. His superiors find it difficult to work out a role for him, so he is kept hidden in the bowels of the building 'helping' with records. He is not allowed to touch anything electronic and the sergeant describes him as a 'human virus'.
>
> The public complain when he is on duty at the station desk. When he is on patrol in the community he has to radio in every thirty minutes and he is not allowed to deal with anything more serious than a request for the time. He is definitely not allowed to direct traffic because he caused 'gridlock' and made the Chief Constable miss his train.

Again, the two answers are almost identical. Notice how briefly this can be done if you focus very clearly on the question. Both answers would get full marks.

Now carefully read the extract on page 13, then complete Activity 2. The extract is from a science fiction novel set in the future. The opening of the story describes the actions of the firemen as they respond to the alarm call. In some ways they seem like firemen today, but in other ways their behaviour is very strange.

The alarm sounded.

The bell in the ceiling kicked itself two hundred times. Suddenly there were four empty chairs. The cards fell in a flurry of snow. The brass pole shivered. The men were gone.

5 Montag sat in his chair. Below, the orange dragon coughed to life.

Montag slid down the pole like a man in a dream.

The Mechanical Hound leapt up in its kennel, its eyes all green flame.

'Montag, you forgot your helmet!'

He seized it off the wall behind him, ran, leapt, and they were off, the night wind
10 hammering about their siren scream and their mighty metal thunder!

It was a flaking, three-storey house in the ancient part of the city, a century old if it was a day, but like all houses it had been given a thin fireproof plastic sheath many years ago, and this preservative shell seemed to be the only thing holding it in the sky.

'Here we are!'

15 The engine slammed to a stop. Beatty, Stoneman, and Black ran up the sidewalk, suddenly odious and fat in their plump fireproof slickers. Montag followed.

They crashed the front door and grabbed at a woman though she was not running, she was not trying to escape. She was only standing, weaving from side to side, her eyes fixed upon a nothingness in the wall, as if they had struck her a terrible blow upon
20 the head. Her tongue was moving in her mouth, and her eyes seemed to be trying to remember something, and then they remembered and her tongue moved again:

'"Play the man, Master Ridley; we shall this day light such a candle, by God's grace, in England, as I trust shall never be put out."'

'Enough of that!' said Beatty. 'Where are they?'

25 He slapped her face with amazing objectivity and repeated the question. The old woman's eyes came to focus upon Beatty. 'You know where they are or you wouldn't be here,' she said.

Stoneman held out the telephone alarm card with the complaint signed in telephone duplicate on the back:

30 'Have reason to suspect attic; 11 No. Elm, City.

E.B.'

'That would be Mrs Blake, my neighbour,' said the
35 woman reading the initials.

'All right, men, let's get 'em!'

Next thing they were up in musty blackness, swinging
40 silver hatchets at doors that were, after all, unlocked.

---

slickers   boots

Activity 2

What evidence is there in these lines that these are not 'normal' firemen and are very different from what we know now? (5)

Remember, you are looking for things that are strange or unusual. The details in the first four lines seem quite 'normal': the men are playing cards and use a fireman's pole. But is there anything unusual about calling a fire-engine an 'orange dragon'? You can answer in bullets or paragraphs.

Examiner tip

Information retrieval
Remember . . .
- Work your way through the suggested lines of the passage.
- Track the text, going through it step by step. Each point you make must count.
- Always stay within the specified lines to find your information.
- Use only information from the text. You could use a highlighter to mark the points you want to use in your answer.

Personal response

What will I learn?

In this unit I will:
- learn to respond effectively to questions that require a personal response to character and relationships
- analyse responses from other students
- practise answering this type of question.

This type of question is asking you to make personal comments on the passage you have read, and to support them with evidence. This means that you should link your comments to words from the text and, when you say something, imagine a voice saying 'prove it'. The focus is on **character** or **relationship** or, occasionally, **a place**.

You should use the first person here (i.e. 'I think that ...') and it is usually sensible to use the wording of the question as a way of getting started. Again, the best approach is to work through the lines of the text specified in the question.

There are three ways in which this type of question can be asked in the exam.

1. What do you learn about a character or relationship?

Your answer to this should begin 'I learn …' or 'The reader learns …' or 'We learn …'.

2. What impressions do you get of a character, or relationship or place?

Your answer to this should probably begin 'I get the impression that …'.

3. What are your thoughts and feelings about a character or relationship?

Your answer to this should include a lot of sentences that begin 'I think …' or 'I feel …'.

'What do you learn?' questions

To get you started, we'll look at an extract and a student's response to a question set on it. The extract below is the opening to a short story called 'Raymond's Run'.

I don't have much work to do around the house like some girls. My mother does that. And I don't have to earn my pocket money by hustling; George
5   runs errands for the big boys and sells Christmas cards. And anything else that's got to get done, my father does. All I have to do in life is mind my brother Raymond, which is enough.
10   Sometimes I slip and say my little brother Raymond. But as any fool can see he's much bigger and he's older too. But a lot of people call him my little brother cause he needs looking
15   after cause he's not quite right. And a lot of smart mouths got lots to say about that too, especially when George was minding him. But now if anybody

has anything to say to Raymond, […] they have to come by me. And I don't play the
20 dozens or believe in standing around with somebody in my face doing a lot of talking.
I much rather just knock you down and take my chances even if I am a little girl with
skinny arms and a squeaky voice, which is how I got the name Squeaky. And if things
get too rough, I run. And as anybody can tell you, I'm the fastest thing on two feet.

There is no track meet that I don't win the first-place medal. […] The big kids call
25 me Mercury cause I'm the swiftest thing in the neighbourhood […] I'm the fastest and
that goes for Gretchen, too, who has put out the tale that she is going to win the first
place medal this year. Ridiculous. In the second place, she's got short legs. In the third
place, she's got freckles. In the first place, no-one can beat me and that's all there is
to it.

30 I'm standing on the corner admiring the weather and about to take a stroll down
Broadway so I can practise my breathing exercises, and I've got Raymond walking on
the inside, close to the buildings, cause he's subject to fits of fantasy and starts thinking
he's a circus performer and that the kerb is a tightrope strung high in the air. And
sometimes […] he'll dash across traffic to the island in the middle of Broadway and give
35 the pigeons a fit. Then I have to go behind him apologising to all the old people sitting
around trying to get some sun and getting all upset with the pigeons fluttering around
them, scattering their newspapers and upsetting the waxpaper lunches in their laps. So
I keep Raymond on the inside of me, and he plays like he's driving a stage coach which
is O.K. by me so long as he doesn't run me over or interrupt my breathing exercises,
40 which I have to do on account of I'm serious about my running, and I don't care who
knows it.

Read the question on this extract, then read the student's
response that follows.

What do you learn about Squeaky in these lines?   (10)

The reader learns a great deal about Squeaky in these lines. First, we learn that she
doesn't 'have much work to do around the house like some girls'. This immediately gives
the impression she is different to most girls her age as Squeaky has no chores. We also
learn that Squeaky's only job at home is to mind her brother Raymond, although this can
be quite difficult.

'All I have to do is mind Raymond, which is enough.'

Squeaky is very protective of Raymond, who appears to be mentally disabled.

'. . . he's not quite right'.

Squeaky is willing to stand up to anyone who makes a comment about Raymond and is willing to 'just knock you down.' We also learn that Squeaky is 'the fastest thing on two feet.' She is serious about her running and winning races so she even practises breathing exercises to prepare for the races. Squeaky is very confident about her abilities and reiterates a number of times that she is 'the best' and that no-one can beat her.

We also learn that Squeaky is in direct competition with a girl called Gretchen, another runner. There is a great deal of rivalry between the girls and Squeaky dislikes her. '. . . she's got short legs . . . she's got freckles . . . no-one can beat me.'

We also learn that although Raymond can be a handful, Squeaky doesn't mind looking after him. He causes havoc by giving 'the pigeons a fit', leaving Squeaky 'apologising to all the old people . . . getting upset'. However, when Raymond behaves and plays quietly, Squeaky doesn't mind.

'. . . he plays like he's driving a stage coach, which is OK by me'.

What did the examiner think?

The student's answer works at two levels. There are details about Squeaky that you can simply pick up from the surface of the text. For example, we learn that she doesn't have to do much around the house. We learn that she is small and skinny, and that she has to look after her brother, Raymond. These are valid points and it is perfectly sensible to include them in your answer, but they do not require much explanation or development. If this was all you did, then you would get a Grade E.

However, this student takes the extra step by interpreting details or reading between the lines. This student makes several good inferences and also uses quotation very well to support her view of Squeaky. This is an A* answer.

Examiner tip

Notice the way the student has used the wording of the question to get started on the answer. This is a helpful approach to answering questions. Notice also where the student has linked the evidence with the comment. It's always useful to have this 'evidence and comment' pattern in your answers wherever you can.

Interpreting details or reading between the lines is called **inference**. You will need to be able to detect inferences in your answers. Inferences are the things we learn about someone or something without being told directly. We work them out for ourselves, by reading between the lines. For example, if someone does the same things at the same time every day, then you might conclude that they are a creature of habit or routine. Similarly, if someone slams their fist on a desk, you probably don't have to be told that they are feeling angry or frustrated. Some inferences are obvious, but others can be subtle. This is why it is so important to read carefully and follow the sequence of the text.

Look at the way the table below assembles the material needed for a good answer to the question on page 16. It focuses on both surface details and inferences.

What is the author trying to tell me?

Surface details	What does this show you? (Inference)
She doesn't have to work around the house.	
She is physically small and skinny.	
She is called Squeaky because of her voice.	
She has to look after Raymond, which she thinks 'is enough'.	Raymond is a chore as far as she is concerned and she finds him a bit of a nuisance.
She does not like what 'smart mouths' say about Raymond and she will just 'knock you down'.	She is protective of her brother and sticks up for him. She is tough and aggressive.
She is 'the fastest thing on two feet' and 'the swiftest thing in the neighbourhood'.	She has a high opinion of her ability. She is confident, even arrogant.
She is nicknamed 'Mercury' by the 'big kids'.	Perhaps she is as good as she says she is (Mercury was the messenger of the gods). She is certainly not modest about running.
She has a rival called Gretchen.	She is very competitive and speaks scornfully about her rival.
She apologises to the old people when Raymond's antics upset them.	She finds Raymond a handful to look after but she can be polite and aware of others.
She takes her running seriously and practises her breathing.	She looks after Raymond but she does not let him distract her from her running.
She lets Raymond run beside her, allowing him to play at stage coaches.	She lets him live in his own little world and as long as he does not bother her, she tolerates him.

Activity 3

Track where the points in the table on page 18 came from in the text (on pages 15–16). Make a note of the line number where each point came from.

Note: it is not always possible to include an inference point – as you can see from the gaps in the table. But there are eight inferences here, as well as at least ten pieces of surface detail and supporting evidence.

Finally, see if you can add at least one extra point, including both surface detail and what it shows you (inference).

'What impressions?' questions

Read the extract below and the questions that follow.
Then complete Activity 4. The extract describes an architect,
Matthew Hall, visiting a potential client called Mr Rutter
for the first time.

There was a high wall, in which was set a pair of double steel gates with, alongside, a bell and entry-phone. Matthew pressed the bell and at the precise same moment a halogen light snapped on and very large dogs began to bark from just inside the gates. The entry-phone quacked.

5 'I can't hear you,' said Matthew. 'On account of those damn dogs. And kindly don't open the gate until someone's got them under control.'

The entry-phone quacked again, and fell silent, unlike the dogs, who continued to bay and presently to fling themselves against the gates. Matthew eyed his car and fingered the keys in his pocket. The gates shook and clanged as the dogs hurled

10 themselves against them and bounced off again. The Post Office presumably visited Mr Rutter by helicopter. After a couple of minutes the baying was interrupted by curses. Some kind of terminal struggle took place, with shouting matched by throaty growls, and the gates swung open. One thickset man in an indefinite uniform (olive green blouson, jackboots, peaked cap) stood there while another was trying to haul away a

15 pair of Rottweilers on steel chains and looking as though he might not succeed.

'Mr Rutter's waiting for you.' […]

'Thanks,' said Matthew. 'I'll just wait till your colleague's got those things out of the way.'

'They wouldn't do nothing.'

20 'I see. Purely ornamental.'

Spotlights blazed onto a garden reduced to alternating sections of grass and paving, with a few glass fibre urns and troughs dotted around. The whole frontage of the house was bathed in a glaring white light. [...] A Rolls with smoked glass windows was parked on the gravel drive up which Matthew and his companion now advanced.

25 The front door stood open. A circular hall, floored in black and white marble, curving staircase with marble balustrade. Much gilt furniture. Large, dark, Italianate oil paintings on the wall. [...]

'Mr Rutter's expecting you in the library,' said the voice, with a hint of impatience. [...] The voice tapped at a pair of panelled doors, paused, opened, and stepped aside,
30 with a nod at Matthew.

It was indeed a library, lined from floor to ceiling with ranks of new-looking, leather-bound editions of this and that. [...] Mostly that. [...] Oriental carpeting. French windows leading to further floodlit sterile expanses of garden.

And Mr Rutter, seated behind a leather-topped desk of gross proportions and
35 tricked out with the appurtenances of modern business – fax machine, VDU, elaborate telephonic arrangements. There was also a large television, let into one of the bookcases.

---

balustrade   ornamental rail
appurtenances   accessories
VDU   computer

The questions asked in the exam on this extract were:

What impressions do you get of Mr Rutter's home? How does the writer create these impressions? (10)

Activity 4

The table below has some of the inferences for the extract on pages 19–20 filled in for you. Copy and complete the table, finding the best evidence you can to support each point. Add any additional inferences that you can find.

This table starts with impressions/inferences, but it does not matter whether you work from evidence to inference, or the other way round. The vital skill is to get used to linking comments and evidence.

What impressions do you get? (Inference)	How does the writer create those impressions? (Evidence)
There is a very high level of security.	
It is very luxurious with obvious signs of wealth.	
It is not homely or welcoming.	
It is tasteless.	
It is full of modern technology.	

Notice that there are about five inferences, or comments, and quite a choice of detail from the text to support these points. An answer that put together both types of information would score very well indeed. It is possible, however, to get an overview of the house, and the best answers might well see that there is something sinister and false about the whole place. Although it has clearly had a lot of money spent on it, it is lacking in warmth and taste. In fact, you would be quite right if you thought that this was a gangster's house, and this might be the inference that turns an answer worth nine marks into one worth ten marks.

Now look at the impressive answer below. This was produced by a student in exam conditions, and it picks up and uses most of the information in the text.

The home of Mr Rutter appears from the description to be a remote hideaway which has tight security as its primary focus. The impression which is immediately in the reader's mind is that the home of Mr Rutter is quite a sinister place. It is a dark and dusty, enclosed space. It is spooky. The writer creates an atmosphere of a highly guarded retreat, where villains can go to ground and wallow in the tawdry luxury of the setting.

The passage opens with a description of the high wall and the double steel gates. Immediately the reader senses that what lurks behind this barricade is furtive and underhand. The barking dogs and the entry phone system offer further validation of the initial impression. The noise of the gates clanging as they open conjures up a frightening vision of old ghost movies and the reader trembles at the prospect of what lies behind the noisy gates and fearsome rottweilers.

The barking rottweilers on their steel chains make the reader want to put their hands over their ears. It is a harsh sound, broken by the glare of the halogen security lights. The harshness of the exterior and the brutal noise which emanates from the outside contrasts strongly with the dark, dusty interior of Mr Rutter's home.

The initial impression is of grand decor but one soon finds it distasteful.

The house is unappealing, decadent, fake grandeur. The circular hall and the black and white marble floor feel pretend, after the brutal lights and barking dogs which we experienced beforehand. The gilt furniture and gloomy paintings portray an image which is of gaudy attempts at a cultured appearance. This feeling is made even more firm when the reader enters the library through the panelled doors and is once more met with attempts at grandeur. The marble statues and oriental carpets sit uneasily alongside the high technology on the desk.

The overall impression of Mr Rutter's home is of a gangster's retreat. The writer creates this impression by carefully taking the reader on a journey from halogen lights, barking dogs and security gates, to a place where dark figures hide away. A place where intruders would be assaulted by rabid dogs and would find nowhere to hide, but where villains, rogues and scoundrels could wallow in illicit splendour.

The claims about the house being 'dusty' are not supported by the passage, but there is a good overview here and the writer works steadily towards the conclusion that there is something false and frightening about the house. It is indeed 'a gangster's retreat', but notice how this student backs up that point with a convincing range of evidence. The answer uses the 'evidence and comment' approach very effectively.

This answer would gain full marks – an A* answer.

'What are your thoughts and feelings?' questions

Read the following extract carefully, then complete Activity 5.

Major Anglesey and Mrs Yardley-Peters worked slowly up and down the aisles of the chain store. They picked up garments and held them against each other. […] Rejecting the blouses and the dressing-gown, they paused at the hosiery counter, where Mrs Yardley-Peters selected three pairs of tights (Brown Haze, Large) and paid for them at
5 the nearest cash desk. They hesitated for a long while over ladies' v-neck lambswool sweaters, eventually deciding on a light grey size sixteen which Mrs Yardley-Peters popped into her shopping bag.
    At Men's Accessories, Major Anglesey held various ties under his chin and decided on a red and navy stripe, which he folded tidily and put in his pocket. From
10 there they wandered to the shoe section. Major Anglesey tried on a pair of brown brogues, took a step or two and shook his head, returning them to the rack. Mrs Yardley-Peters, meanwhile, had put on some black pumps – size four since, although a stout woman and not short, she had surprisingly small feet. The Major nodded approval and Mrs Yardley-Peters slipped her own
15 shoes into her shopping bag, keeping on the pumps. Major Anglesey, at this point, glanced at his watch, said something, and the two of them moved rather more quickly to the food department where they filled a wire basket with a carton of coleslaw, two portions of cooked chicken, a packet of jam fancies and a jar of powdered
20 coffee, lining up with those at the checkout. […]
    Major Anglesey and Mrs Yardley-Peters passed through the checkout and back into the main part

of the shop. At the entrance, they stopped for a moment, Mrs Yardley-Peters being evidently fussed in case she had lost her gloves; a search of her handbag, however,

25 apparently put things right, and they proceeded under the blast of tropical wind issuing from somewhere in the ceiling and out into the street.

30   The store detective caught up with them at the zebra crossing, as they stood waiting for a lull in the traffic. She asked if they would please

35 come back to the manager's office. The Major and Mrs Yardley-Peters received this request with considerable surprise but made no

40 objection, except that the Major looked again at his watch and said he hoped it wouldn't take too long, as it was getting on for lunch-time.

pumps   trainers

Answer the following question.

What are your thoughts and feelings about Major Anglesey and Mrs Yardley-Peters?   **(10)**

To help you get started, note that the first few lines describe the couple looking at clothes in a shop and then paying for three pairs of tights. What impression does this give you of them? What happens next? What do you think now?

Now complete your answer.

Use 'I think …' and 'I feel …', and support your points with reference to the extract. You need to make clear what effect the text has on you as a reader, and, as always, it is sensible to start at the beginning and work your way carefully through the lines.

Activity 6

This is your opportunity to demonstrate what you have learnt in this section: it's time to try this type of question on your own!

The extract below describes a group of Army recruits arriving at a training camp, Catterick, in Yorkshire for the first time. Read it, then answer the question that follows.

Our truck ground and whined through a seemingly endless expanse of squat huts huddled together round bleak parade grounds, forbidding barrack blocks, dejected rows of married quarters, and everywhere obtrusive military notice boards, with their strident colours and barbaric language of abbreviations. […]

5 We always seemed to be moving our belongings at Catterick from one part of the camp to another. It started on the first afternoon when, after the cursory medical, we were issued with knife, fork, spoon, mug and bedding. A mattress, I found, was a peculiarly awkward thing to carry, since it was impossible to get one's arms round it in any way. Eventually, after dropping the mattress once, and

10 smashing my mug in the process, I stumbled into a hut and flung my burden down on a vacant bed. I quickly tossed my blankets on to the next bed to keep it for Mike.

I sat on the bed and inspected the inhospitable interior of the hut. The floor was of uncovered stone flags. Several panes were missing from the windows.

15 There was a low, battered tin locker beside each bed. Two deal tables and a few chairs made up the rest of the furniture. In the middle of the hut, at some distance from my bed, was a small, ineffective-looking stove. I was glad it was still August. […]

When Mike came in and deposited his bedding, we followed a bunch of

20 Regulars to the cookhouse, a dark, high-roofed cavern, echoing with the clash of cutlery and the noisy mastication of sausages, mashed potatoes and gravy. It was a meal I found peculiarly repulsive at that hour, particularly the gravy, which I was too slow to intercept as it splashed onto my plate. […]

An officer in a black dress uniform, with highly polished belt and buckles,

25 moved among the weary conscripts as they sat shovelling sausages and mash down their gullets. A sergeant with a black sash paced watchfully at his heels, as if he were conducting the officer through some zoo of cowed but potentially dangerous animals.

obtrusive attention-grabbing
deal wooden

What impressions do you get of the conditions in Catterick Camp? (10)

Remember to use evidence from the text and to link it to your comments.

Character response

What will I learn?

In this unit I will:
- learn the techniques used to respond effectively to questions that require exploration of a character's thoughts or feelings
- analyse responses from other students
- practise answering this type of question.

This type of question changes the focus of your answer and requires you to show your understanding of a character's thoughts, feelings or actions. You have to approach this type of question with a clear sense of sequence. This means going through the text line by line in a logical order (since the writer chose to write the story in a particular order, it seems sensible to follow it). This is what teachers and examiners mean when they talk about being 'methodical' in answering a question. You should use the third person – in other words, you should start most of your sentences with 'He …', or 'She …' or 'They …'.

There are four ways in which this type of question may be asked in the exam.

1. **What are the character's thoughts and feelings?**
   Your answer should include a lot of sentences that begin 'He or she thinks …', 'She or he feels …' or 'They think/feel …'.

2. **What is going through a character's mind?**
   Your answer should include a lot of sentences that begin 'He is thinking …' or 'She is thinking …'. It is particularly important to establish a sense of sequence in your answer. People tend to think in a logical order and your answer should follow the thought process of the character.

3. **How does a character react, behave or change?**
   Answers to this sort of question also focus on the responses of a character, but you need to be careful with this question.
   - 'How does a character *behave* …?' is fairly straightforward and requires you to focus mainly on the character's **actions**.
   - 'How does a character *change* …?' suggests something different and you need to be alert to developments in the character.
   - 'How does a character react …?' requires you to look at what they **do**, **say**, **think** and **feel**. In other words, you need to cover that character's actions, thoughts, words and emotions.

4. Why does a character act or behave in a certain way?
This type of question is asking you to understand the behaviour of a character and **explain** the reasons for their actions.

'What are the character's thoughts and feelings?' questions

Let's have a look at the way these questions work. Read the extract below and the question that follows it. The extract is about a teenage girl who lives with her father, her stepmother and her half-brother. She is finding her home life quite difficult.

Paula was trying to write an essay entitled 'The Use of Irony in *Cold Comfort Farm*'. She had to finish it by the end of term but she hadn't even started it yet. Home was so chaotic, that was why. The house was so small with Barnaby in it. Simone, her stepmother, was training to be a psychotherapist and she liked to have quality time
5 with Barnaby when she got home. This meant that Barnaby didn't get to bed till late and spent the evenings screaming around the house, pretending to be a fighter jet. He liked launching himself from the settee and landing on Paula's stomach. Wherever she spread out her notes, the cat sat on them. Then there was her father, padding around because he had writer's block, making himself cups of tea and engaging everyone in
10 conversation but scuttling away the moment Barnaby approached. […]
      Simone was much younger than Paula's Dad – only thirty-two. She was beautiful in all the ways Paula wanted to be – like being thin, with masses of of black hair that somehow looked sexy and wild, whereas Paula's just looked a mess. When she moved in she said she didn't want to be a stepmother type of person, she wanted to be Paula's
15 friend, her confidante, just girls together. She said if ever Paula wanted to talk, she would be there. She said *talk* in a special way, a capital letters way, that filled Paula with unease and somehow made the walls of the house close in around her.
      The trouble with Simone was that she was too understanding. She understood Paula's feelings
20 about her mother, who had run away to Totnes with a man who made stained-glass windows. She understood about being plump because she said – unbelievably – that she too had once had a weight problem. She understood about being
25 an adolescent because she was still practically one herself, and besides, she had written a paper called 'Psychodrama and the Teenage Dynamic'. What she didn't understand was the main point of being seventeen, which was to be misunderstood.
30   'If only she was older,' Paula said to her friend Kate. 'I want her to be like a parent.'

What are Paula's thoughts and feelings about her home and family? **(10)**

Your answer will need to cover Paula's thoughts and feelings about home, of course. In dealing with her family, you need to think about her half-brother, Barnaby, her dad and also her stepmother, Simone. The surface details in the text can be used as evidence to support the inferences that you include in your answer.

The table below assembles the material for an answer to this question.

Surface details (Evidence)	Paula's thoughts and feelings (Inferences)
Home is 'chaotic'.	She thinks there is no peace or privacy in which to work.
Paula thinks the house is 'small' with Barnaby in it.	She feels she has no space and there is no discipline or control of him.
She hasn't even started her essay.	She tells herself this is because she finds it difficult to work at home.
Barnaby goes to bed late and spends the evenings screaming around the house, pretending to be a fighter jet.	She thinks he is a noisy nuisance. She perhaps feels a little jealous or pushed out, as Barnaby seems to come first.
Her father is constantly making cups of tea and starting conversations.	She thinks her dad is also a distraction and gets in the way. He avoids work.
Her father 'scuttles' away from Barnaby.	She also thinks her dad avoids responsibility.
She is filled with 'unease' by Simone, who understands all the problems of teenagers.	Simone is too young and too understanding.
Simone doesn't understand that teenagers need to be 'misunderstood'.	She is not like a 'proper' parent.

Activity 7

The table above lists eight possible points, each of them tied to some support from the text. Your task is to organise the material into a really good answer, written in paragraphs, to the question at the top of this page.

You will need to make five or six inferences to get full marks here. Each inference must be supported by evidence from the text.

'Why does a character?' questions

Read the extract and question on page 29, then do Activity 8 on page 30. The extract is about a student (who was working as a waitress in a coffee shop) who almost loses her life when she agrees to take part in a test run of a raft on the rapids beneath Niagara Falls.

When she was twenty-one, Emma nearly died. Or so she was told, and since four of those with her actually did die, she had to believe it. At the time she hadn't felt anywhere near dead.

5 It was a freak accident, and the fact that she was there at all was an accident too, the result of a whim and of knowing someone. Emma always knows a lot of people. The person she knew for this occasion was a man, a boy really, about her own age. He didn't qualify as a boyfriend, he was just one of the group she'd hung out with the previous year, at university. In the summers he worked for a travel agency, a good one that specialised in organising out-of-the-ordinary tours: bicycle 10 trips through France, African game parks, that sort of thing. This boy, whose name was Bill, was one of the tour leaders. […]

Bill was a nice boy, nice enough so that when he ambled into Emma's coffee shop one day and told her that he wanted her body, Emma took it as a joke and did not resent it. Really he wanted her to come on a test run, he said. The travel 15 agency he was working for was doing a pilot project on a new kind of tour: down the Whirlpool Rapids below Niagara Falls on a big rubber raft. They'd done the run nine times so far, and it was perfectly safe, but they weren't ready to open the tour to the public until they'd had one more test. […] It struck him as the kind of thing that might appeal to Emma.

20 Emma was flattered by this image of herself, and readily accepted it as a true one: a physically brave young woman, a bit of a daredevil, willing to put on a life jacket at a moment's notice and sit on a large inflated platform of rubber and swirl down the dangerous Niagara Whirlpool Rapids. It would be like roller coasters, which she'd always found compelling. She would join the ranks of 25 those who had in the past, wished to challenge Niagara Falls: the tightrope walkers, and those who'd had themselves bolted into padded barrels and flung into the river above the drop, even the suicides, whom Emma lumped in with the challengers, because if you were not in some way gambling, why not just use a gun? […]

30 Emma said yes at once and arranged for her next day off to coincide with the tenth rubber-raft test run. On the morning of the day, which was a Monday, Bill picked her up from the run-down frame house she rented with three other girls and drove her across the Rainbow Bridge to the launching site, which was on the American side. It turned out afterwards – some reporter dug it up – that 35 the Canadian officials had refused permission, considering the enterprise too hazardous, but even if Emma had known this it probably wouldn't have stopped her. Like many of her countrypeople, she considered her fellow Canadians a lacklustre bunch.

Why does Emma take part in the test run of the raft? (10)

The question is testing your understanding of Emma's motives and the circumstances that led to her agreeing to take part.

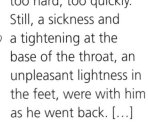

Activity 8

1. Working on your own, list as many relevant points as you can to answer the question on page 29. Try to find at least ten reasons why Emma took part in the test run.
2. Now, working in pairs, compare your lists. Decide what to keep and what to leave out.
3. Finally put away all the notes and lists, and produce your answer as a timed task in 12 minutes.

'What is going through a character's mind?' questions

The extract below describes the reactions of Stephen Lewis, who is shopping in a supermarket with his three-year-old daughter, Kate. He has just noticed that she has gone missing while he is at the checkout.

Unhurriedly he pushed the trolley clear, thinking she had ducked down behind the end of the counter. Then he took a few paces and glanced down the only aisle she would have had time to reach. On one side there were lines of shoppers, on the other a clear space, then the chrome turnstile, then the automatic doors onto the pavement. There

5 may have been a figure in a coat hurrying away from him, but at that time Stephen was looking for a three-year-old child, and his immediate worry was the traffic.

[…] As he shouldered past shoppers and emerged onto the broad pavement he knew he would not see her there. Kate was not adventurous in this way. She was not a strayer. She was too sociable, she preferred the company of the one she was with.

10 She was also terrified of the road. He turned back and relaxed. She had to be in the shop, and she could come to no real harm there. He expected to see her emerging from behind the lines of shoppers at the checkouts. It was easy

15 enough to overlook a child in the first flash of concern, to look too hard, too quickly. Still, a sickness and

20 a tightening at the base of the throat, an unpleasant lightness in the feet, were with him as he went back. […]

25 At a controlled run – he was not yet past caring how foolish he looked – he went down all the aisles, past mountains of oranges, toilet rolls, soup. It was not until he was back at his starting point that he abandoned all propriety, filled his constricted lungs and shouted Kate's name.

Now he was taking long strides, bawling her name as he pounded the length of an
30 aisle and headed once more for the door.

The question on this extract is:

What is going through Stephen's mind in these lines? (10)

The focus of the question is Stephen and what he is thinking as he realises his daughter is missing. You need to work through the lines, suggesting what is in his mind and linking your comments to evidence from the text.

> **Remember**
>
> Skimming and scanning are useful reading techniques. **Skimming** is used to obtain the gist (the overall sense) of a piece of text. **Scanning** is used to obtain specific information from a piece of text.

Activity 9

Pick out key words or phrases from the extract on pages 30–31, then copy and complete the table below. This will help you to assemble your answer.

Each of your comments in the left-hand column should be matched by at least one piece of evidence in the right-hand column. You need to identify about six 'steps'.

What is he thinking?	How do you know? (Evidence)
At first he thinks his daughter is behind the counter or has wandered down the nearest aisle.	He pushes the trolley aside 'unhurriedly' and 'glances' down the aisle (no sign of any panic).
He then becomes more concerned and thinks she might be on the road.	

'How does the character react?' questions

The extract below describes a situation in which an elderly woman has been persuaded to allow a group of schoolchildren to paint her kitchen. Read the extract, then answer the question that follows.

'Hi,' a boy with long blonde hair said to her on the Tuesday morning. There were two other boys with him, one with a fuzz of dark curls all round his head, the other red-haired, a greased shock that hung to his shoulders. There was a girl as well, thin and beaky-faced chewing something. Between them they carried tins of paint, brushes,
5 cloths, a blue plastic bucket and a transistor radio.

'We come to do your kitchen out,' the blonde boy said. […]

She let them in, saying it was very kind of them. She led them to the kitchen, remarking on the way that strictly speaking it wasn't in need of decoration, as they could see for themselves. She'd been thinking it over, she added: she wondered if
10 they'd just like to wash the walls down, which was a task she found difficult to do herself?

They'd do whatever she wanted, they said, no problem. They put their paint tins on the table. The red-haired boy turned on the radio. […]

'Would you like some coffee?' Mrs Malby suggested above the noise of
15 the transistor.

'Great,' the blonde boy said. […]

Mrs Malby made them Nescafé while they listened to the music. […] She smiled at the girl. She said
20 again that it was a job she couldn't manage any more, washing walls. […]

Mrs Malby closed the kitchen door on them, hoping they wouldn't
25 take too long because the noise of the transistor was so loud. She listened to it for a quarter of an hour and then decided to go out and do her shopping.

How does Mrs Malby react when the children arrive to paint her kitchen? **(10)**

Notice that the text focuses on the reactions of Mrs Malby as opposed to the children. The word 'react' means that you need to address what she does, what she says, what she thinks and what she feels.

Let us start by tracking her 'reactions'.

- She let them in.
- She said it was very kind of them to come to paint her kitchen.
- She led them to the kitchen.
- She said that 'strictly speaking' her kitchen did not need painting.
- She said she'd been thinking it over.
- She suggested they might just wash the walls.
- She said she found this job difficult.
- She offered them some coffee.
- She smiled at the girl.
- She repeated that washing the walls was difficult for her.
- She closed the door to block out the noise of the radio.
- After a while, she went out to do her shopping.

This kind of 'tracking', working through the text step by step, would get you a long way in answering this type of question. This is the textual evidence on which you must base your answer. However, to get more than six or seven marks, you would need to draw some conclusions. (This is called making inferences or reading between the lines.)

Activity 10

1. In pairs, look at the words in the box and decide which ones are good descriptions of Mrs Malby's reactions.

rude	trusting	threatening
concerned	hostile	tactful
suspicious	pleased	aggressive
reluctant	polite	pleasant

2. Now decide which of Mrs Malby's 'reactions' (from the list above) you could link to each of the words you have chosen.
3. On your own, try to produce a good answer in no more than 15 minutes.

Activity 11

Now try approaching a text and preparing yourself to answer a particular type of question. This time you are on your own!

The extract below describes a group of British soldiers in World War I who are waiting for the order to launch an attack on enemy trenches. Read it, then answer the questions that follow. Both questions are based on the same material but the change in their wording alters your 'angle of approach'.

The barrage was due to start in fifteen minutes' time. Prior shared a bar of chocolate with Robson, sitting hunched up together against the damp cold mist. Then they started crawling forward. The sappers, who were burdened by materials for the construction of the pontoon bridge, were taking the lane,
5 so the Manchesters had to advance over the waterlogged fields. The rain had stopped, but the already marshy ground had flooded in places, and over each stretch of water lay a thick blanket of mist. Concentrate on nothing but the moment, Prior told himself, moving forward on knees and elbows like a frog or a lizard or like – like anything except a man. First the right knee, then the left, then
10 the right, then the left again, and again, and again, slithering through fleshy green grass that smelled incredibly sharp as scrabbling boots cut it. Even with all this mist there was now a perceptible thinning of the light, a gleam from the canal where it ran between spindly, dead trees.
   There is to be no retirement under any circumstances. That was the order.
15 They have tied us to the stake, we cannot fly, but bear-like we must fight the course. The men were silent, staring straight ahead into the mist. Talk, even in whispers, was forbidden. Prior looked at his watch, licked dry lips, watched the second hand crawl to the quarter hour. All around him was a tension of held breath. 5.43. Two more minutes. He crouched down further, whistle clenched
20 between his teeth.

sapper   a soldier who erects bridges

1. **What thoughts and feelings do you experience as you read these lines?** (10)

2. **What thoughts and feelings do Prior and his men experience as they wait for the order to attack?** (10)

The craft of the writer

In this unit I will:
- learn the techniques used to analyse the ways in which writers create particular effects
- analyse answers from other students
- practise answering this type of question.

Writers use a range of techniques to create character, or atmosphere or emotion. This is your opportunity to show that you understand how they do it.

The four types of question

There are four ways in which this type of question can be asked in the exam.

1. How does the writer convey, create, make or suggest?

This type of question is asking you to analyse how writers create particular effects. The question will always ask you about a specific effect, but remember the focus is on 'how does the **writer**' rather than 'how does a **character**'. For example, you could be asked how a writer creates tension, excitement, drama, uncertainty, horror and so on. There are three areas to look at.

a. You should consider the effect of **content**. This is *what happens* in the specified lines of a passage and you should not ignore it.

b. You should also consider the effect of **language**. This involves commenting on *the effect on the reader* of particular words and phrases, including the use of figurative language.

c. If you can, you should also think about the **structure** of the passage. This is thinking about *how the story has been organised*, or put together. It might also involve commenting on some of the narrative techniques writers use such as viewpoint, dialogue and flashback.

2. What happens in these lines? How and why do you react to what happens?

This type of question often, but not always, refers to the conclusion and will usually be asked when the storyline is not completely obvious. The question is testing your understanding of the narrative, and you need to identify the key actions and events in the specified lines to show that you know what is going on.

However, there is always more to this question than just summarising the sequence of events. 'What happens' may also include some development in the main characters or in the themes of the story.

You will often be asked to include your personal response to 'what happens'; this requires you to describe your thoughts or feelings as the story unfolds.

3. How effective is the ending?

This type of question is perhaps the most difficult. It focuses clearly on the ending of a passage or story and asks you to evaluate its success, or lack of it!

> **Examiner tip**
>
> **Feature-spotting**
>
> The questions in your GCSE English exams are not about simply identifying parts of speech such as adverbs, or literary devices such as similes. It's good if you know the difference between an adverb and an adjective or a simile and a metaphor. However, merely spotting these features will not increase your marks. You must try to comment on the effect of particular uses of language, and a response like the one below should be avoided.
>
> *The writer creates drama by using third person and a lot of adjectives.*
> *There is an effective simile in line 71.*
> *The writer uses short sentences except where they are long.*
> *The writer uses a lot of superlative adjectives such as you and me.*
>
> These comments are vague and, even when they are 'correct', they are unnecessary. You must identify specific examples of any features you spot, and comment on how they work.

Some endings are predictable, answering all the questions and tying up all the loose ends. This type of ending provides you with all the information you require as a reader. For example, a detective story would be frustrating if you did not find out 'whodunit' in the last few pages.

Some endings do the opposite – they deny you information. This can be the 'cliff-hanger' ending much loved by soap operas, not least because they want you to watch the next instalment. However, when the end of a story is a cliff-hanger, the writer is deliberately challenging you to create the ending. These 'open' endings leave you with unresolved questions.

Another type of ending takes you by surprise with an unexpected or ironic twist. This kind of ending is usually well concealed until the last minute, and often there is a build-up of tension or suspense.

One way of evaluating endings is to ask yourself how, and why, an ending leaves you feeling the way you do. Writers will often attempt to provoke an emotional response on the part of the reader: happiness, sadness, horror, amusement or a range of feelings.

> **Examiner tip**
>
> With this type of question, it's useful to deal with a short section of the text, maybe just a few lines. Explain how you react to what has happened – your thoughts and feelings – at that point in the story. Repeat this pattern as you work through the text. This will allow you to explain precisely how your thoughts and feelings change as the story develops.

4. What are your thoughts and feelings as you read these lines?

This type of question simply asks you to say how you are thinking and feeling. But you must remember that the wording does not focus solely on character. You need to include your response to the characters and also to the way the story's plot or themes are developing.

'How does the writer convey?' questions

Look at how you might approach this type of question. Read the extract below, which continues the story – written by Margaret Atwood – from page 29. Then complete the activity that follows. A young woman has agreed to take part in a test run of a raft on the rapids near Niagara Falls. She thinks it will be exciting and fun, but she is almost killed when things go badly wrong.

> But once they moved out into the current, the rubber surface under her began to ripple, in large waves of contraction, like a giant throat swallowing, and spray came in upon them, and Emma knew that the rapids, which had looked so decorative, so much cake frosting from a distance, were actual after all. There were some dutiful
> 5 thrilled noises from the other passengers, and then some genuine noises, less thrilled. Emma found herself clutching Bill's arm, a thing she wouldn't ordinarily have done. [...]
> There was a lot of talk later about why the tenth run should have failed so badly, after the other nine had gone without a hitch. [...] All she saw was the front of the
> 10 raft tipping down into a trough deeper than any they'd yet hit, while a foaming wall of water rose above them. The raft should have curved sinuously, sliding up the wave. Instead it buckled across the middle, the front half snapping towards the back, like the beak of a bird closing. Emma and Bill and the other people in the front row shot backwards over the heads of the rest, who were jumbling in a heap at the bottom of
> 15 the V, now submerging. [...]
> Something struck her on the side of the head – a foot in a boot, perhaps – and she was underwater. Later she learned that the raft had flipped and a man had been trapped underneath it and drowned, so it was just as well that she had been flung clear. But underwater she did not think. Something else made her hold her breath
> 20 and struggle towards the surface, which she could see above her, white and silver, so her eyes must have been open. Her head rose up, she gasped air and was sucked under.
> The water tumbled and boiled and Emma fought it. She was filled almost to bursting with an energy that came from anger: *I refuse to die in such a stupid way,*
> 25 was how she formulated this afterwards. She thinks she shouted at least once: 'No!'

Which was a waste of breath, as there was nobody around to hear her. There were rocks, and she collided with several and was bruised and scraped, but nothing more hit her head, and after what seemed like an hour, but was really only ten minutes, the current was less and she found she could keep her head above the water and actually
30 swim. It was hard to move her arms. She propelled herself towards the shore, and, finally, dragged herself up onto a small rocky beach. Her running shoes were gone. She must have kicked them off, though she couldn't remember doing it, or maybe they had been torn off. She wondered how she was going to get over the rocks without shoes.
35 The sky was even bluer than it had been before. There were some blue flowers also, weeds of some kind, cornflowers, growing among the rocks. Emma looked at them and did not feel anything. She must have been cut, her clothes were certainly ripped, there was a lump on the side of her forehead, but she didn't notice any of this at the time.

Activity 12

The way to approach this type of question is to look line by line at the specified section picking out the details of language and context which convey the sense of drama.

So, let's practise this form of close reading. First, read the exam question that could be asked on the extract on pages 37–38:

How does the writer convey the drama of the accident? **(10)**

Now, in pairs, discuss and make notes on the questions and tasks below.

1. What is the first sign of trouble?
2. Find three other pieces of evidence in the first paragraph that suggest that people are becoming frightened.
3. What happens to the raft and the other people on it?
4. Pick out some of the words and phrases that make the action seem fast-moving and dramatic.
5. What is the simile in the extract? Explain the effect of that image.
6. Look at what happens to Emma. Can you pick out the events and the words and phrases that make this exciting?
7. When she finally gets to the shore, what state is she in? How do you know?

You should now have the basis of a good answer to the exam question.

The two student answers below use the extract on pages 37–38 to answer the question below.

How does the writer convey the drama of the accident? **(10)**

Answer 1

> She conveys the drama by using short sentences or long ones with a lot of detail. Lots of describing words to create a more realistic atmosphere.
>
> A lot of action happens in these three paragraphs and she writes about it. Well, she keeps you interested. The way she writes makes it seem like you're there. It's very realistic and makes you want to read on.

Examiner tip

In this type of question, it's useful to begin some of your sentences with 'The writer ...', then go on to explain what the writer (rather than the character) is doing. Opening some sentences like this will help you to focus on the question and stop you slipping into just re-telling the story.

Answer 2

> The writer conveys the drama of the accident in a descriptive, stative and straightforward way which actually makes the story quite gripping and easy to read.
>
> The accident starts off in a sense of distress and unease as Atwood tells us that the 'rubber surface under her began to ripple . . . were actual after all.' The sense of danger then increases as Atwood explains that the 'dutiful thrilled noises' soon turn to 'genuine, less thrilled' noises. This may grip the reader and get them to carry on reading with more interest.
>
> Atwood often adds little details about what happened to the raft in the end, before the story gets to that part eg 'there was a lot of talk later about why the tenth run should have failed so badly'. This intensifies the story as it states that something very bad happens to the raft and it adds wonder to the story and again gets the reader to read on to get the action.
>
> Then straight after the clue, Atwood tells us of how the raft goes into a huge trough and a 'foaming wall of water rose above them.' The atmosphere is very tense now as the reader realises that the people are in danger.

Activity 13

1. In pairs, discuss the strengths and weaknesses of each of the student responses on pages 39 and 40. Record your findings in a table like the one below.

	Strengths	Weaknesses
Answer 1		
Answer 2		

2. Using the passage on pages 37–38, write your own response to the question below in not more than 15 minutes.

   How does the writer convey the drama of the accident? (10)

   Make this your own response rather than copying the ideas in the example student answers!

Empathetic response

What will I learn?

In this unit I will:
- learn to write as if I am a character from the passage, selecting the key details and focusing on the character's thoughts and feelings
- analyse responses from other students
- practise answering this type of question.

'Empathetic response' questions appear in the English exams, and also in the English Literature exam, so it is worthwhile knowing how to tackle them well.

They require you to imagine that you are a character in the story and to give that character's version of events. They test your understanding both of the story and the character. You have to imagine that you are that character and ask yourself how they would feel about the events.

Sometimes you may be asked to write in the form of a diary. At other times you may be asked to imagine you are telling a neighbour or a friend what has happened. In either case, your answer must be based on a careful reading of the passage.

There are some key points that you must keep in mind as you tackle this type of question. Above all, think about the following.
- What would the character know?
- What would be important to the character?
- How would the character react to events?

Examiner tip

Make sure your answer actually deals with the events in the passage. This is not an opportunity for creative writing.

Improving your diary answers

If you can catch the 'voice' of the character by trying to sound like them, then that will improve your answer. But the key to answering this type of question is to show detailed understanding of the events and the way the character would think and feel about them.

Read the following extract. It is about a fifteen-year-old girl called Sadie who asks her parents if she can have a party at home.

'Can I have a party?' Sadie said, with no preamble.

'A fine time to ask,' Ben said, 'when your mother has just got back from an exhausting trip.'

'That's all right,' Angela said quickly. 'Of course you can have a party. I've always
5 loved your parties.' And she had – for years she had given Sadie wonderful parties, imaginative and well organised, the envy of the neighbourhood. Sadie winced. 'The only thing is,' she said, 'I'd like to do it myself this time – I mean, I wouldn't want you there.'

'That sounds like a good idea,' Angela said carefully.

10 'I don't want the boys either. I'd like the house empty. I couldn't have the sort of party I want with the boys here – it spoils it.'

'How does it spoil it?'

'I don't want to go on about it – I just want the house empty. Can't you take them away somewhere?'

15 'For your convenience?'

'Okay, okay. Forget it. I won't have a party. It doesn't matter.'

'Don't be petty – of course you can have one – it's just I don't see how I can get rid of three boys without a great deal of bother. Couldn't I just guarantee that they all stay on the top floor?'

20 'For God's sake don't try and persuade her,' Ben said.

'I suppose so,' Sadie said, grudgingly. 'But there'll be a lot of noise – they might not

sleep – it wouldn't be any good them complaining. And you're not going to say no drinking or smoking are you?'

'Certainly I am,' Ben said.

25 'What kind of party is this?' Angela said.

'Just the kind everyone has. I'd clear up the mess and everything. You wouldn't have to do anything. But I need the house.' […]

'I could cook pizzas,' Angela offered.

'No,' Sadie said, 'it would be a waste of time. They'd only get stood on. I don't want
30 any proper food.'

'And I don't want any proper drink,' Ben said.

'Beer's harmless,' Sadie said, 'and cider and a fruit punch – I can have that can't I?'

'I suppose so,' Angela said.

'I'll clear the ground floor,' Sadie said, 'and we won't let anyone go upstairs. Where
35 can I put the lampshades and pictures and big things like rugs?'

'But why do you have to move lampshades?'

'They might get broken – it's best to have as little stuff about as possible. It's for your sake, you know – it's your things I'm protecting.'

Activity 14

The extract on pages 42–43 should give you a view of Sadie and her relationship with her parents.

In pairs, find evidence to show the following.

1. Sadie wants a party but wants her parents to have no involvement in it.
2. Sadie's parents react in different ways when she asks to have the party.
3. Sadie can be a bit pushy and wants to get her own way.
4. She can be aggressive and sulky with her parents.
5. Sadie's mum (Angela) tries to keep the peace between Sadie and her dad.

The exam question on this extract would require you to turn what you know about Sadie and her parents into a diary entry, making it sound as though she is actually writing it.

Before trying it yourself, look at the following student's attempt, produced in exam conditions, at writing Sadie's diary based on this extract.

Answer 1

> Today I asked mum if I could have a party like all the others are having at school, with no parents and loads of drink and smoking. At first I thought she would say no but she said it was OK and she didn't really mind about the damage and mess as long as I cleaned it up.

What did the examiner think?

Answer 1 is not a strong response. The student seems to have some understanding of what happened, but fails to mention Dad completely. There is a little awareness of how Mum reacted, but there is no real attempt to show how Sadie was thinking or feeling. It's a short, weak answer, likely to achieve a Grade G/F, but it could easily be improved by:

- reading carefully through the text
- deciding what is important to Sadie
- noting how she reacts to her parents' responses
- writing the diary the way you think Sadie would do it.

Now look at another student's response to the same extract, also produced under exam conditions.

Answer 2

> I've just asked Mum and Dad for my party. Well, this was difficult, as I knew Dad was going to come out with his lectures and I would have to cut down on the party. Again Dad sarcastically gave his remarks, 'No smoking', 'No alcohol'. It's ridiculous. I shouldn't have bothered asking if they were going out – they're staying on the top floor. At least they aren't patrolling the area and I can have the boys out of the way.
>
> At last Mum came to the rescue. I knew she would help me get through this one. I wouldn't know what to do without her. Mum let me have as many people as I wanted. Mum has always let me do whatever I liked. It's just Dad who comes in the way and spoils it. Dad makes me feel caged and I sometimes wonder why I bother. Mum doesn't mind what I do.

Answer 2 is a much stronger piece of work because:

- we get a clear view of how Sadie feels about both her parents
- useful details from the story are included in the answer such as what Dad said, parents staying on the top floor
- we get a real sense of Sadie's frustration with her dad.

This is a good answer that makes sensible use of the details in the story. But what makes this a Grade C response is the way it captures Sadie's character – the way she reacts to her parents' concerns and the way she talks about her dad.

Activity 15

Now that you have seen these two student responses, try writing a diary entry for Angela (Sadie's mum), based on the extract on pages 42–43.

Remember:
- you should write in the first person ('I …')
- Angela will have a different view of events from Sadie.

Improving your understanding of characters

Read the following extract. The exam task here is to imagine that you are Mrs Malby and you are telling your best friend about what happened.

'We're trying to help them,' he said, 'and of course we're trying to help you. The policy is to encourage a deeper understanding between the generations.' […]
    'Well, of course it's very kind,' Mrs Malby said. […]
    He said:
5   'What age actually are you, Mrs Malby?'
    'I'm eighty-seven.'
    'You really are splendid for eighty-seven.'
    He went on talking. […]

'So what I thought,' he said, 'was that
10 we could send the kids on Tuesday. Say
start the job Tuesday morning, eh, Mrs
Malby?'

'It's extremely kind of you.'

'They're good kids.'

15 He stood up. He remarked on her two
budgerigars and the geraniums on her
window-sill. Her sitting-room was as warm
as toast, he said; it was freezing outside.

'It's just that I wondered,' she said,
20 having made up her mind to say it, 'if you
could possibly have come to the wrong
house?'

'Wrong? *Wrong?* You're Mrs Malby,
aren't you?' He raised his voice. 'You're
25 Mrs Malby, love?'

'Oh, yes, it's just that my kitchen isn't
really in need of decoration.' […]

He said, quite softly, what she'd
dreaded he might say: that she hadn't
30 understood.

'I'm thinking of the community, Mrs Malby. I'm thinking of you here on your own
above a greengrocer's shop with your two budgies. You can benefit my kids, Mrs
Malby; they can benefit you. There's no charge of any kind whatsoever. Put it like this,
Mrs Malby: it's an experiment in community relations.' […]
35 'It's just that my kitchen is really quite nice.'

'Let's have a little look, shall we?'

She led the way. He glanced at the kitchen's shell-pink walls, and at the white
paintwork. It would cost her nearly a hundred pounds to have it done, he said; and
then, to her horror, he began all over again, as if she hadn't heard a thing he'd
40 been saying. He repeated that he was a teacher, from the school called the Tite
Comprehensive. […] The man repeated what he had said before about these children:
that some of them came from broken homes. The ones he wished to send to her on
Tuesday morning came from broken homes, which was no joke for them. He felt, he
repeated, that we all had a special duty where such children were concerned.
45 Mrs Malby again agreed that broken homes were to be deplored. It was just, she
explained, that she was thinking of the cost of decorating a kitchen which didn't need
decorating. Paint and brushes were expensive, she pointed out.

'Freshen it over for you,' the man said, raising his voice. 'First thing Tuesday,
Mrs Malby.'

---

deplore   pity or disapprove

There is a lot to read here and your answer has to include a mixture of:

- what you (Mrs Malby) would tell your friend about the visit from the teacher
- how you (Mrs Malby) feel about the teacher and how he behaved.

Here is a list of points you might possibly have made about the visit:

- the teacher was from a local school and he wanted to send his children to paint your kitchen
- he said the children were from broken homes and it would help them
- you didn't think the kitchen needed re-decorating but he insisted, saying there was no charge
- he was going to send them on Tuesday.

You should also be able to show how Mrs Malby *felt* about her meeting with the teacher.

Activity 16

In pairs, note down the feelings and thoughts you might have had if you were Mrs Malby. For example:

At first I thought he was being kind because he wanted to help children.

Before you imagine yourself as Mrs Malby talking to your best friend, read the following answers written by students under exam conditions.

Answer 1

A man came and knocked on my door. He said he was a local teacher and was helping some kids who were from broken homes. He said that some kids would be round Tuesday morning to decorate my kitchen. I said, 'My kitchen does not need decorating.' He then started talking about how he would help me and how he was thinking of the community. He was trying to persuade me to let some children in to decorate my kitchen. I asked if he had the wrong house and he started getting angry and raised his voice in frustration.

What did the examiner think?

Answer 1 only tells us what happened and there is very little about Mrs Malby's thoughts and feelings. It does not say anything about the way she reacted when the teacher said her kitchen could be re-decorated. It would not gain many marks – and would be viewed as a Grade G/F response.

Answer 2

Maggie, you will not believe what happened today. On Monday afternoon I got a knock at the front door. I thought it was a salesman at first but it was a teacher from the local school telling me I could have my kitchen decorated by some of his pupils because they are from broken homes. Well, of course you want to help if you can. He seemed to be kind but . . . you know . . . pushy. He didn't seem to listen to me. I told him it didn't need doing but just ignored me. I thought he might have come to the wrong house but he just kept repeating my name as if I was daft so in the end I let him blab on. He kept on and on about how I'd be helping these kids. Then he came in the kitchen, looked at it in disgust and told me he would send his kids round today.

What did the examiner think?

Answer 2 uses some parts of the story quite well; it includes the details about the teacher and the reason for the visit but this response also begins to explore Mrs Malby's feelings, hinting that she may have felt a little intimidated by the way he seemed to treat her. The answer could have explored in more detail the way Mrs Malby's feelings about him change during the conversation. Also, towards the end, what is being said does not really sound like Mrs Malby; there is an occasional word or phrase that seems out of keeping with the way she talks in the passage. Although there are some aspects of the passage that could be developed in greater detail, this is certainly an improvement on Answer 1 and would be viewed as a D grade response.

Activity 17

This task is your opportunity to show that you have learnt how to tackle 'empathetic' questions.

Write down what you think Mrs Malby would tell her best friend. You would have about 12 or 13 minutes to complete this task, so your answer should be between half a side and one side in length.

Remember:

- your answer should include what happened but must also concentrate on your thoughts and feelings
- you should write in the first person
- you must select points that would be important to Mrs Malby
- you should try to sound like Mrs Malby.

What have I learnt?

In this section we covered:

- techniques for locating and retrieving information from a text
- responding effectively to questions that require a personal response to character and relationships
- learning to write like a character from the passage, selecting the key details and focusing on the character's thoughts and feelings
- techniques used to analyse the ways in which writers create particular effects
- types of Paper 1 Section A exam questions.

How confident do you now feel about each of the above? You could note down the points you feel confident about and those you need to go back to.

Introduction

What will Section A of Paper 2 look like?

In Section A of Paper 2 you will have to read two examples of non-literary texts on a common theme. These could be an advert, a newspaper or magazine article, a page from the Internet, a leaflet or an essay (e.g. travel writing).

Each year the exam includes different texts in different combinations, so you cannot predict what will be used. Also, it is highly unlikely that you will have read the material before.

What will the questions be like?

As with Paper 1 Section A, the questions fall into different, but quite predictable, categories. The trick is to recognise the type of question and what it requires. You need to prepare yourself by practising the types of questions you are likely to be asked and you should use a range of different kinds of material. For example, a leaflet is different from an essay, and you need to be confident about how to approach the various kinds of material. This section of the book is designed to help you to do exactly that.

The wording of the questions varies from year to year and you cannot be certain which questions will appear. However, only **seven** basic types of question are asked in this exam. Examples of these appear on page 51. If you practise answering them, then you should be well prepared and able to face the exam with confidence.

What should I do?

You have around 50 minutes to complete this section of the paper, so there is no time to waste. First, you could read the two texts. This will take some time so, alternatively, you could just read the text you need to answer the opening one or two questions. You then only need to read the second text when you reach the question(s) on that text. Only the last question will ask you to consider both texts.

Paper 2 Section A sample question types

Below are some examples of the types of question you could be asked in Section A of your Paper 2 exam. These will help you to understand what you are preparing for as you work through this section of the book.

1. Locating and retrieving information
- List reasons or details/Make a list of …
- According to this text or writer, how or what or why … ?
- Explain how and/or why …

2. Impressions and images
- What impression do you get of the writer/an organisation/people?
- What image does this text create of the writer/an organisation/people?

3. Viewpoint and attitude
- What are the writer's attitudes to … ?
- What are the writer's opinions of … ?
- What are the writer's thoughts and feelings about … ?

4. Intended audience
- Who is this text aimed at?

5. Analysis of persuasive techniques
- How does the writer try to encourage/interest/argue?
- How does this text try to persuade/sell/influence?

6. Comparison of texts
- Compare and contrast these texts.

7. Evaluation of texts
- Which of these texts do you find more effective?

Locating and retrieving information

In this unit I will:
- learn to select the relevant details from a passage and present them in a clear way
- practise answering this type of question.

Questions that ask you to locate and retrieve information are usually opportunities to gain marks quickly, provided you read the passage carefully and closely. If this type of question appears, it is usually the first question in Paper 2. Often you will simply be asked to list five or ten relevant details from the passage.

'List' questions

Read the following extract from an article about an encounter with polar bears in Canada.

Examiner tip

If you are asked to 'make a list' or 'list …', then you should do exactly that. If you are asked for ten points, include eleven or twelve if you can. You may have got something wrong or made the same point twice, but an extra point or two gives you a safety net.

Help! It's the scare bear bunch

When 200 bears pay an annual visit, it's time for the people of Churchill – polar bear capital of the world – to keep their heads down. Peter Baumgartner reports. […]

Churchill is the polar bear capital of the world; every year, in November, the town's 1000 inhabitants have to share their living space with 200 of them. The bears invade Churchill while waiting for Hudson Bay to freeze over so that they can hunt on the ice for seals, their favourite food. Just before winter begins in earnest, Churchill has a
5 six-week 'season', and adventure tourists from around the world make for the Arctic Circle to watch them. But droll and clumsy as they look, polar bears are among the most dangerous predators on earth. Fast, strong and unpredictable, they weigh up to 600kg and attack without warning.
　　Denise, our guide, cautions me at once when I try to photograph a warning sign
10 that reads, 'Polar bear alert. Stop. Don't walk in this area.' The notice is at the edge of town in front of a few rocks. Behind it is the slowly freezing bay. 'That is not a good

idea!' she snaps, pulling me back. She has twice seen a bear appear suddenly from behind the rocks.

What do you do in such cases?

15   'Take your clothes off and slowly walk backwards,' she laughs. 'Bears are naturally curious. They stop at each garment and sniff it. You must never just run away, and you must never look them directly in the eyes. That annoys them. The best thing is gradually to make for the nearest house.' In Churchill, house doors are supposed to be unlocked all the time for just such emergencies. [...]

20   If someone sees a bear in the closed zone of town, they call the polar bear police, and the rangers come and knock it out with an anaesthetic gun. The sleeping white giant is placed in transit detention at the polar bear jail.

At the jail, we find just two bears under lock and key. There is space for 32. Last year the rangers caught and freed 108 bears. When the jail is full its inmates are flown out 25 20 or 30 miles to the north.

---

droll   amusing

The question on this extract is:

List ten details from the article that suggest polar bears are dangerous.   **(10)**

The extract contains a lot of details that answer this question. Even in the introduction there is a suggestion that people avoid the bears – it says that they 'keep their heads down'. This would earn a mark. In the first paragraph, there are five details that suggest they are dangerous animals.

Your answer could be written as a bullet point list, as below.

- They are 'among the most dangerous predators on earth'.
- They are fast.
- They are strong.
- They are unpredictable.
- They weigh up to 600kg.

Each of these points would gain you a mark. But be careful: you may also have been tempted to include as a separate point the fact that the bears 'attack without warning'. But this suggests they are unpredictable – and you will have already been rewarded for this point. When you answer this type of question, you will often be able to simply copy the relevant details, as you would have done above. Sometimes, though, you may need to put the answer into your own words.

In the second paragraph, the tour guide explains the need for caution. The key point in this paragraph that suggests bears are dangerous is that they appear suddenly at the edge of town. To gain a mark here, you would need to put this in your own words – for example 'they can appear suddenly at the edge of town'.

Activity 1

Look again at lines 15–22 in the article on page 53. Find and list another three points that suggest polar bears are dangerous.

Activity 2

Below are the final paragraphs of the article that began on page 52. Read through the text and list any details that suggest polar bears are dangerous.

The next morning we drive in a 'tundra buggy' (a converted bus with giant wheels) to the Wapusk National Park, out in the monotonous, treeless and endlessly flat tundra. The region is like Siberia, and GIs once fought war games here. We almost miss our first bear: he lies whitely dozing on the permafrost. 5 Getting out of the vehicle now would be deadly. His looks can be misleading: a polar bear can manage a speed of 50km/h and he can kill with just one swipe of his massive paw. So feeding is forbidden. The occupants of a smaller buggy ahead of us are 10 already scared. One of the bears has reared up and is sniffing at the vehicle. His mouth easily reaches the slightly open window. The tourists pull back, horrified, but the bear is only sniffing. His nose 15 is his most important tool: with it, he can smell seals under a metre-thick ice cover.

By the second day of our buggy tour, the bears love 20 us. First of all two males give an impressive wrestling bout lasting for several minutes, but they are only playing. Either could kill the 25 other with no difficulty at all. They are so near that we can see their sharp teeth and claws with our telephoto lenses. And then we see a female with a pair of cubs 30 about two months old. They have killed a bird and are chewing the feathers.

On the way back we see how the bears from the polar bear jail are flown out. Anaesthetised, they hang in the net below the helicopter that will take 35 them back to the tundra. Hopefully they won't wake up before they are released to freedom.

There are a number of points that could be made here about how dangerous polar bears are. How many could you find? When added to all the previous points, you can see that you have more than ten.

Activity 3

Now it's time to practise this type of question on your own. Read the following extract, about a 93-year-old man called Fauja Singh who runs marathons.

He maintains a steady, moderate pace like a man entirely in control of himself and his destiny. He likes routine and he runs nine or 10 miles a day, every day,
5   clocking up 70 miles a week. There is nothing particularly unusual about that, you think – there are plenty of people who take their training seriously – until you discover that this man is 93 years
10   old. […]
     He looks the picture of health. When I saw him, he ran several laps of his pavement circuit – exactly 2.147 km – at 15 minutes each and with no rest
15   in between other than a few swigs from a bottle of water waiting for him on a wall. He was not even breathless.

Answer the following question:

List five things you learn about the way Fauja Singh prepares for marathons. (5)

Impressions and images

In this unit I will:
- learn how texts attempt to present an impression or image of their subject
- analyse responses from other students
- practise answering this type of question.

'What impressions' questions

Sometimes a question is asked in Paper 2 about what **impression** an article or a factsheet creates of an organisation, an individual or a group of people. This simply means the kind of view you might have of the person or organisation when you read what is being said about them.

Read the newspaper article below, then complete Activity 4.

The sunshine isle where teenage tearaways are sent to learn a lesson

With its cooling palms and spectacular views of the nearby mountains, it is an idyllic holiday destination.

This Caribbean paradise is also the
5 playground of a group of notorious teenage tearaways.

While their hard-working classmates shiver in the cold and rain back home, the seven are spending two weeks in the sun,
10 enjoying swimming, tennis and trips to the sights of Jamaica, as part of a scheme organised by the Divert Trust.

The five boys and two girls, aged 13 to 16, who come from Nottingham are
15 considered the most disruptive pupils at their three schools.

All face expulsion after consistently skipping classes, disrupting lessons,
disobeying teachers and breaking school
20 rules.

Many failed to do their homework or show any commitment to school work and school activities.

'Nobody knows what to do with them,'
25 a school governor said last night. 'But sending them on a free holiday is not the answer.'

'What kind of message does this give out to other children when they see the
30 way these children have been given such a special treat?'

The youngsters are staying at a former hotel built in 1888 in a suburb of the capital Kingston and now used as a Roman
35 Catholic convent and school complex for 1400 children.

Just a few miles away are soft white beaches lapped by the bluest of oceans.

40 The Divert Trust, a charity which offers support to children at risk from school exclusion, has footed the full £5000 bill for the trip 45 and claims it will be 'highly beneficial'.

Chief executive Angela Slaven insisted yesterday: 'They will have to study at 50 schools, talking to people and experiencing how children in Jamaica learn. This is certainly not a holiday.'

The pupils have a full 55 programme of events for their stay, which includes visits to schools and cultural institutions.

The organisers hope what they see will encourage them to value their 60 education and respect authority after seeing how Jamaican children are committed to their school work, despite the fact that many have few resources and live in poverty.

65 The tearaways will also enjoy days out at the Dunn's River Falls tourist attraction and a museum dedicated to reggae legend Bob Marley.

Outraged parents and governors 70 condemned the venture as an insult to better-behaved classmates.

A governor at the school which two of the seven attend, said the school was 'very annoyed' at the decision to take them 75 away.

She added: 'We were not informed about the trip and we hadn't sanctioned it. I really didn't agree with almost rewarding badly-behaved children.'

80 At the convent, run by the Missionary of the Immaculate Conception, the children are closely supervised but are still able to enjoy the expansive grounds and playing fields.

85 Sister Celia Cools-Lartigue said: 'They are enjoying their stay. They are a bit noisy at times but otherwise not too bad.

'They have a packed schedule every day and will be taking lots of trips.

90 'They sleep in dormitories and have two good meals a day. They seem to be fussy eaters, though – we don't really know what to feed them. They don't seem to like English or Jamaican food.'

95 The trip was originally aimed at 19 pupils who were set individual targets for achievement, but only seven performed well enough to secure a place.

Activity 4

The writer creates a negative impression of these teenagers. Having read the article on pages 57–58, list any words or phrases in the first 20 lines of the article that help to create this impression, and say what image they suggest. For example, the use of the word 'tearaways' in the headline suggests they are out of control.

This article appears to be a report about an organisation that is trying to help some teenagers who are struggling at school. But as you read it, did you begin to have a view about these children? Did you start to think they didn't deserve the kind of help and support they were being given?

When you look more closely, it becomes clear that this article is not just reporting facts; it is trying to influence the reader's view, both of the children and the charity that organised their trip. It is trying to create a particular impression of the teenagers, and it does this by the careful choice of words and phrases in the article and the way the facts are reported.

You need to be able to spot the words and phrases that make you think about the teenagers (or the organisation) in a particular way, and say what impression it creates of them.

Now let's consider an exam question:

What impressions does this newspaper article create of the seven teenagers on the Divert Trust scheme? How does it create these impressions? **(10)**

Look at the article's headline. By using an emotive word like 'tearaway', the writer is already creating an impression of what the teenagers are like. To answer the question effectively, you need to look at the following.

- What the article tells the reader about these children – for example, they are described as 'notorious' and 'tearaways'. These words immediately give an impression of children who don't behave well, challenge authority and have a bad reputation.
- How the article presents the information – for example, in the third paragraph the scheme is described as 'two weeks in the sun, enjoying swimming, tennis and trips to the sights of Jamaica'. This makes it sound more like a holiday, especially when the teenagers are contrasted with 'their hard-working classmates' who will have to 'shiver in the cold and rain back home'. This use of contrast helps to create an image of undeserving teenagers whose bad behaviour seems to have earned them a luxury holiday!

Activity 5

Using the article on pages 57–58, copy and complete the table below. This will help to focus your reading of the passage and make you alert to **what** is said about the teenagers and **how** it is said.

What impressions do we get of the teenagers?	What details from the passage give us this impression?
They are troublemakers/unruly.	'notorious teenage tearaways'
	'the *most* disruptive'
No respect for authority/rude/horrible.	
	no interest in school work and school activities

This will give you all the material you need to answer the question. But, before you attempt your own answer, look at what one student produced under exam conditions.

The newspaper article describes the seven teenagers as 'a group of notorious teenage tearaways'. From this statement we are immediately given the impression that these children are always up to no good and don't think about the consequences of their actions. The article goes on to explain that they are the 'most disruptive' and 'all face expulsion'. This does not make the seven pupils sound as if they deserve a holiday as one governor has pointed out 'a free holiday is not the answer'. Everything that is said about the seven teenagers or 'tearaways' does not create a good impression and many people are said to be outraged. This makes the article sound quite aggressive and it reflects badly on the teenagers. The writer often refers to them as 'tearaways', 'disruptive' and 'badly behaved'. These references are constantly keeping up the bad impression we are given of them. Even the Divert Trust scheme is said to be 'a charity which offers support to children at risk from school exclusion'. This does not commend the charity, but highlights that these children have behavioural problems.

What did the examiner think?

This answer begins sensibly with a direct reference to the teenagers, and the opening sentences keeps a tight focus on the question. The comment that follows ('these children are always up to no good') also gains reward, but the answer then becomes rather repetitive and towards the end loses its focus on the teenagers almost entirely; there is nothing to reward in the final sentences. Overall, it misses a lot of the details. It gets a Grade C.

The candidate picks up some of the points you will have included in your table, and it was sensible to begin by working through the article from the beginning. However, the answer 'tracks the text' much less carefully after the opening three sentences and misses a lot of the detail that you will have included in your table.

Activity 6

Use the details and impressions you have collected in your table to write an answer to this question about the passage on pages 57–58:

What impressions does the newspaper article create of the seven teenagers on the Divert Trust scheme? How does it create these impressions?

You have seen that working carefully through the text helps you to select the evidence you need for your answer. Once you have the evidence, you have the opportunity to add your own comments, which strengthens your answer and will certainly be rewarded by an examiner.

You should try to use this approach whenever you are asked a question about the impression or image an article is trying to create.

Examiner tip

Remember that in an exam, even if you have lots of points to make, you must still complete the answer in about 12 minutes.

Viewpoint and attitude

What will I learn?

In this unit I will:
- learn how texts attempt to present a viewpoint or attitude towards their subject
- analyse responses from other students
- practise answering this type of question.

'Attitudes' questions

You will have seen from the newspaper article in the previous section that writers often do more than present facts and information; they frequently want to present a particular view on the subject they are writing about or persuade the reader. They may have a negative or positive attitude towards their subject, and sometimes an exam question will ask you to explain what their attitude is and how this is made clear to the reader.

A question of this sort is likely to contain the word 'attitude' or 'viewpoint' in it, but you might simply be asked to explain the writer's 'thoughts and feelings'.

Read the extract on pages 63–64, by the American writer Bill Bryson. It was written following his return to America after living for many years in Britain.

Junk food heaven

Some weeks ago I announced to my wife that I was going to the supermarket with her next time she went because the stuff she kept bringing home was – how can I put this? – not fully in the spirit of American eating. Here we were living in a paradise of junk food – the country that gave the world cheese in a spray can – and she kept bringing
5 home healthy stuff like fresh broccoli and packets of Ryvita.

It was because she was English, of course. She didn't really understand the rich, unrivalled possibilities for greasiness and goo that the American diet offers. I longed for artificial bacon bits, melted cheese in a shade of yellow unknown to nature, and creamy chocolate fillings, sometimes all in the same product. I wanted food that squirts
10 when you bite into it or plops onto your shirt front in such gross quantities that you have to rise carefully from the table and limbo over to the sink to clean yourself up. So I accompanied her to the supermarket and while she was off squeezing melons and pricing shiitake mushrooms I made for the junk food section – which was essentially all the rest of the store. Well, it was heaven.

15 The breakfast cereals alone could have occupied me for most of the afternoon. There must have been 200 types, and I am not exaggerating. Every possible substance that could be dried, puffed and coated with sugar was there. The most immediately arresting was a cereal called Cookie Crisp, which tried to pretend it was a nutritious breakfast but was really just chocolate chip cookies that you put in a bowl and ate with
20 milk. Brilliant. […]

I grabbed one of each of the cereals and two of the oatmeal – how often I've said that you shouldn't start a day without a big steaming bowl of cookies – and sprinted with them back to the trolley.

'What's that?' my wife asked in the special tone of voice with which she often
25 addresses me in retail establishments.

I didn't have time to explain. 'Breakfast for the next six months,' I panted as I dashed past, 'and don't even *think* about putting any of it back and getting muesli.'

I had no idea how the market for junk food had proliferated. Everywhere I turned I was confronted with foods guaranteed to make you waddle, most of which were
30 entirely new to me – jelly creme pies, moon pies, pecan spinwheels, peach mellos, root beer buttons, chocolate fudge devil dogs and a whipped marshmallow sandwich spread called Fluff, which came in a tub large enough to bath a baby in. […]

Aisle seven ('Food for the Seriously Obese') was especially productive. It had a whole section devoted exclusively to a product called Toaster Pastries, which included, among
35 much else, eight different types of toaster strudel. And what exactly is toaster strudel? Who cares? It was coated in sugar and looked drippy. I grabbed an armload.

I admit I got a little carried away – but there was so much and I had been away so long.

It was the breakfast pizza that finally made my wife snap. She looked at the box and
40 said, 'No.'

'I beg your pardon, my sweet?'

'You are not bringing home something called breakfast pizza. I will let you
have' – she reached into the trolley for some specimen samples – 'root beer
buttons and toaster strudel and . . .' She lifted out a packet she hadn't noticed before.
45 'What's this?'

I looked over her shoulder. 'Microwave pancakes,' I said.

'Microwave pancakes,' she repeated, but with less enthusiasm.

'Isn't science wonderful?'

'You're going to eat it all,' she said. 'Every bit of everything that you don't put back
50 on the shelves now. You do understand that?'

'Of course,' I said in my sincerest voice.

And do you know she actually made me eat it. […]

The most awful of all was the breakfast pizza. I tried it three or four times, baked it
in the oven, zapped it with microwaves, and once in desperation served it with a side
55 of marshmallow Fluff, but it never rose beyond a kind of limp, chewy listlessness. […]

Which is why, when I came across it again the
other day, I regarded it with mixed feelings. I
started to chuck it out, then hesitated
and opened the lid. It didn't smell bad
60 – I expect it was pumped so full
of chemicals that there wasn't
any room for bacteria – and I
thought about keeping it a
while longer as a reminder
65 of my folly, but in the end
I discarded it. And then,
feeling peckish, I went off
to the larder to see if I
couldn't find a nice plain
70 piece of Ryvita and maybe
a stick of celery.

The exam question on this extract was:

**What are Bill Bryson's thoughts and feelings about
American food? You must use the text to support
your answer.**   (10)

The easiest way to begin this question is by 'collecting the
evidence' – in other words, to look closely at what the writer
actually says about American food. You will find that Bryson's
view changes through the extract, and tracking the change
through close attention to exactly what he says is the key to
gaining high marks on the question.

By working your way carefully through the text you are already starting to build up the material you will need to produce a good answer. The points that could be made, looking only at the first part of the extract (up to line 20), could be presented as follows.

Bill Bryson's thoughts and feelings about American food	Evidence from the text
He is keen to get back to eating American food, which is different from British food. He is not put off by the fact that American food is not very healthy.	He talks about being in 'junk food heaven' – 'heaven' suggests food he really adores. He calls America a 'paradise of junk food'.
He does not want his wife to buy healthy food / He is not interested in healthy food.	His English wife brought home 'healthy stuff', like fresh broccoli and Ryvita, which was not what he wanted. He seems to mock his wife for the attention she gives to vegetables – 'squeezing melons'
At first, he thinks (or pretends to think) all American food is wonderful. He 'longed for' the unusual, artificial nature of American food and the bizarre combinations of foods on sale.	He loves food that has 'possibilities for greasiness and goo'. He could not wait to eat a product that combined 'artificial bacon bits' with unnaturally yellow cheese and creamy chocolate filling.
He gets excited about the messy foods and the huge quantities involved. The unhealthier the foods sound, the more he wants them. His excitement seems child-like and perhaps ironic. He seems to want to buy everything that he sees.	He wanted food that 'squirts when you bite into it' and would 'plop' onto his shirt 'in gross quantities'.
He likes the way most of the store is given over to 'junk food'.	He again calls this 'heaven'.
He is impressed by the vast choice on offer.	There were '200 types' of breakfast cereals, which would have 'occupied' him 'for most of the afternoon'.
He knows Cookie Crisp only pretends to be healthy – but he is impressed by the sound of it.	He calls Cookie Crisp 'immediately arresting' and 'brilliant'.

Notice that you may be able to use a number of examples of supporting evidence for a comment you make. Don't be frightened to do this; it will show the examiner how carefully you are probing the text. Also notice that on some occasions you will be able to use and comment on just part of a sentence or even the impact of a single word – for example, the use of the word 'heaven'.

Examiner tip

Using and commenting on just part of a sentence or even the impact of a single word will be rewarded by the examiner because it shows the ability to select evidence carefully.

Activity 7

1. Using only the material that has been collected into the table on page 65, write, in paragraphs, the opening part of your answer to the question:

What are Bill Bryson's thoughts and feelings about American food? You must use the text to support your answer.

Tips for doing this well
- Try to make sure your answer uses sentences that link the writer's attitude towards American food to the evidence.
- It can also be helpful to use part of the title to begin sentences, for example: 'Bill Bryson's thoughts and feelings about American food are clear from the title …'
  Or:
  'Bill Bryson also thinks American food is …'

2. When you have finished your version, work in pairs or groups to see how you have used the details.
   a. Do all the versions contain the same information?
   b. Which is the longest piece?
   c. Are there parts of the answer that don't include details from the grid?

Activity 8

1. Working in pairs, create a table of Bill Bryson's thoughts about American food and the evidence to support these points, for the rest of the extract (from line 21 to the end).

Points to remember as you are completing this task
- Make sure that everything you write down is answering the question.
- The evidence you collect might be part of a sentence or could just be a single word.

2. When you have completed your table, work with another pair to compare your work. Discuss the differences in your tables and add anything to your version that you think you have missed.

By creating this table, you now have lots of material that you could add to the answer you began in Activity 7. Before completing your own answer, read the answer on the following page, written by a student in examination conditions:

Bill Bryson's wife is English and she doesn't like his junk food as she 'was not fully in the spirit of American eating'. This quote tells us that he enjoys his food, junk food. She didn't understand the rich, unrivalled possibilities for greasiness and goo that the American diet has to offer.

Bryson likes food that makes a mess when you eat it – 'food that squirts when you bite into it or plops onto your shirt in gross quantities'. We know he adores junk food because when he went into the supermarket with her, he headed to the junk food section and described it as 'heaven'.

As he put some Cookie Crisp into the trolley he said 'and don't even think about putting it back and getting muesli'. Muesli is a healthy cereal and this quotation shows his dislike for healthy food.

Bill Bryson also buys toaster pastries, even though he didn't know what it was. He bought it because it was coated in sugar. Unhealthy.

But at the end, Bill Bryson's wife makes him eat all the junk food he bought and he thought it was awful. The marshmallow Fluff was 'limp, chewy listlessness'. He felt like a fool. Then he went and got a plain piece of Ryvita or a stick of celery when he was peckish. This shows us that he hates junk food because he ate too much. He'd rather stick to the healthy food.

Activity 9

Imagine you are marking this student's answer.

Working in pairs, decide how good the student's answer is. In order to do this you should work through each paragraph in turn, jotting down your comments as you go, with the following in mind.

- Is the point being made answering the exam question? For example, does the student always focus on the thoughts of Bill Bryson?
- When quotations are used are they explained effectively?
- Does the student comment on the impact of individual words or phrases?
- Does the student miss out valuable points from the extract that should have appeared in their answer?
- Does the student spot the key change in Bill Bryson's thoughts and feelings?
- Does the student develop the points they made in the answer?
- Does the student notice some of the techniques that Bill Bryon uses, such as humour or exaggeration?

Finally, decide what grade the student's answer deserves overall.

All the work you have done, and seen, on this text should give you a clear idea of what an examiner is looking for in a question on viewpoint and attitude.

Activity 10

Now you are ready to complete the following question:

What are Bill Bryson's thoughts and feelings about American food? You must use the text to support your answer.

You have already completed your answer on the first part of the extract, in Activity 7. Now you need to complete your answer, in paragraphs, on the remainder of the extract (line 21 to the end). You can use the table you created on this section, in Activity 8, if you wish.

Remember

Timing your work is very important. You should aim to complete a full answer to a question in this section of the exam in no more than 12 minutes.

Intended audience

In this unit I will:
- learn how texts target particular individuals or groups of people
- practise answering this type of question.

Questions on intended audience are not often used in the exam, but they can be asked, usually in relation to advertisements. Some students are quick to claim that adverts appeal to 'everyone'. Occasionally this may be true, but advertising is not usually aimed at the entire population.

In fact, advertisers are very skilful at aiming their advertisements at particular audiences and they target potential consumers in a number of ways. They think of people in categories, not least because advertising is expensive and they want value for money. They think carefully about where and when they advertise their products, and they target their audience in terms of things such as:
- age
- gender
- income
- interests.

If you are asked a question about intended audience, you will need to work out who the specific targets are by looking at content and language.

Let's look at an example.

Where memories are made of sea, sand and fun

No childhood is quite complete without remembered dreams of halcyon days spent at the seaside, paddling in the waters or playing on the sands.

Llandudno has two beaches on either side of the town. The quieter West Shore with its long sandy beach and children's play area has wonderful views of the Conwy Estuary, Isle of Anglesey and Puffin Island, site of a Cistercian monastery.

North Shore is the lively beach, spanning the two-mile crescent bay for which Llandudno is famed.

Its popularity has stood the test of time. The traditional still thrives in the form of Punch and Judy shows, donkey rides and organised games. On the Pier there are stalls and amusements including Professor Peabody's Playplace with supervised activities for children. On the opposite end of the promenade, at Craig-y-Don, toddlers love splashing about in the paddling pool.

The promenade itself is a hive of activity during the glorious months of summer. There are fun events such as the charity pram race and bed-making competitions. The waiter and waitress race, a keenly-fought title by the town's hotels, is in its 26th year. On balmy summer evenings listen to the sounds of local or visiting bands on the bandstand.

For fun and frivolity, sunbathing and people-watching, Llandudno is truly the place where memories are made.

Neighbouring Llanfairfechan, a small coastal resort town, is an excellent starting point for energetic walks as it is surrounded by woodlands, mountain scenery and seascapes. There's a long safe open stretch of sand and visiting yachtsmen are welcome at the Sailing Club. There are opportunities for angling, riding, windsurfing or to play a round of golf on the town's nine-hole course.

AT A GLANCE

Angling	Sea fishing from the pier all year round. Day tickets available at the pier. Tel: (01492) 876258
Bait	Available from Kiosk by the Pier or from 'Llandudno Fishing Tackle', Craig-y-Don. Tel: (01492) 878425.
Boat Trips	Half-hour trips around Great Orme's Head depart frequently from the jetty, North Shore Promenade, May–September. Tel: (01492) 877394.
Fishing Trips	Organised by boatmen at Conwy and Llandudno. Contact the Harbour Master for further details. Tel: (01492) 596253.

Llandudno North Shore and Llanfairfechan are *Tidy Britain Seaside Award Winners*.

This advertisement is obviously trying to attract visitors to the seaside resort of Llandudno. Your task is to work out exactly whom they are trying to attract.

You will notice that the pictures show children playing on the beach, enjoying donkey rides, and watching a Punch and Judy show. It would be tempting to jump to the conclusion that the advert is aimed at children, until you think that small children do not actually make decisions about where to go for a day out or a holiday. A more accurate answer would be that this advert is aimed at parents, or families, with young children.

Activity 11

Look at the first four paragraphs of text in the leaflet on page 70.

1. Make a list of the activities that would attract parents and young children.
2. Pick out any words or phrases you think are particularly effective.

The photographs reinforce the appeal to parents with young children, and your answer should include some reference to them. This is the most important audience for this advert, but it does have other targets.

Activity 12

1. Paragraphs 5 and 6 mention some 'fun events', including the 'waiter and waitress race' and 'people-watching'. Who do you think might be interested in those activities?
2. The final paragraph, which begins 'Neighbouring Llanfairfechan', is aimed at another group of people. Who exactly are they? What is mentioned to appeal to them?
3. Now look at the section on the bottom of the advert with the heading 'At a Glance'. Who is this section appealing to? How does the advert do this?

You should have identified at least four groups of people who are targeted by this advert, but it is definitely not aimed at 'everyone'. The group that is most obviously missing here is teenagers – there is really nothing to appeal specifically to them!

Analysis of persuasive techniques

What will I learn?

In this unit I will:
- learn the techniques used to analyse the ways in which writers try to influence readers
- learn the various forms of persuasion
- analyse answers from other students
- practise answering this type of question.

Persuasive writers can use a variety of techniques, and the exam questions will almost certainly require analysis of how a particular text is attempting to influence its audience. It could be selling a product or promoting an idea or a point of view, but writing is never really neutral, particularly this kind of writing.

As you read each text, try to establish a sense not only of its topic (what it is about) but also of the writer's viewpoint (what the writer really thinks about the topic).

The questions are likely to be worded as follows:

- How does the writer try to encourage, or interest or argue?

or:

- How does this text try to persuade, or attract or sell or influence?

You should consider the following points as you are working through your answer:
- approach
- content
- language
- structure
- tone
- headlines and titles
- pictures
- presentation.

Try to learn this checklist for the exam. We will now look at each point in turn.

Examiner tip

The best way to proceed is to 'track' the text, taking each paragraph or section in turn. The most important thing is to ask yourself: 'What is the intention behind this detail?', 'What is the effect?'

Remember

This is intended to be an analysis of how a writer tries to persuade. It is not asking whether you agree or not. You must look at what the writer is doing and resist the temptation to give your own views on the issue.

Examiner tip

The question is *not*: 'How does the writer make you want to read on?' So don't answer that question instead of the actual one!

Approach

Think about the underlying approach being used and how the writer tries to influence the reader. This is your opportunity to stand back and analyse the bigger picture. Sometimes this is called 'overview', and it is really about the tactics a persuasive writer uses to put across an argument.

For example, arguments are won in the following two ways.

1. Pointing out the benefits or advantages or what is to be gained (the positive case):
   - for the individual (you in particular)
   - for others
   - for society
   - for the environment.

2. Pointing out the dangers or disadvantages or what could be lost or attacking your opponents (the negative case):
   - for the individual
   - for others
   - for society
   - for the environment.

An argument may focus on personal, social, environmental or moral issues. It may appeal to self-interest, or our social or moral concerns. It may appeal to our better nature, give clear instructions, or use commands or orders (imperatives) politely!

Emotional responses are common features of persuasive writing. They can include:

- scare tactics (playing on your fears or insecurities)
- shock tactics (often sensational or creating outrage)
- an appeal to your hopes, dreams or ambitions
- an appeal to your vanity or snobbery
- an appeal to your better nature or idealism
- an appeal to your self-image.

An argument can be put 'positively', but it can be 'negative' in undermining or contradicting the opposition. Often, persuasive writing will combine these two approaches. Try to think about the 'underlying tactic' beneath the surface detail.

Sometimes writers will use personal or first-hand experience to give weight to what they are saying. Interviews and quotations may be important.

Read this extract written by a student, then complete the task that follows.

Food for thought – are we a nation of fatties?

What did your children have for lunch today? Ask them. Go on. Actually, you don't have to bother. I can tell you. Chips were probably
5 involved, a fizzy drink of some sort, a greaseburger or some other deep-fried delicacy. This is, of course, a huge generalisation, and to those who do go for salad or
10 spaghetti bolognese, I apologise.

However, the sad fact is that we have bad eating habits because that's what we've always known. We eat fatty, fried foods in school and it sets the pattern for later life. We need to change this, but how?

How many of you have been to a fast food restaurant this week? Come on,
15 don't be shy. Too many are doing this in Britain. There's no excuse for it. It's not the cheapest option, and I'm prepared to bet it's not the tastiest either. We all know the risks, but we shrug our shoulders and carry on our path of artery-clogging destruction. Why not go to a healthier food store? Heck, bring your own sandwiches, but don't do this to yourselves, people! Some of you reading this
20 article, right now, could die as a result of your eating habits. Stop now. Cease this madness! The McDonalds salads are your enemies too. They're just as fattening so don't be fooled by the marketing ploy. We all know what's healthy and what's not, so let's do something about it.

List the 'tactics', e.g. shock tactics (see the list on page 73), that this writer uses. For each tactic in your list, include at least one piece of evidence.

Content

This is a very important feature of any text. Almost all questions will focus on content to some extent, even the 'how' questions.

Think about:
* facts and opinions (what is said, the selection of material, the points writers choose to suit their purpose)

A fact is something that is always true and cannot be argued with, such as 'Madrid is the capital of Spain'.

- the arguments used by the writer
- the use of examples
- the use of statistics or figures
- the use of quotations (often by experts or personalities such as Jamie Oliver, Billie Piper or Chris Martin to give 'celebrity endorsement' and encourage others to follow their example).

Identify the features you think have an effect. Consider why they are there and the effect they achieve. Find and mention the underlying techniques, but always back them up with specific examples from the text and explain what effect they have.

The title of the article below, 'Boiling the Frog', seems to suggest quite clearly what the article is about. In fact, it is about the writer's claim that motorists are being persecuted and slowly 'boiled' by the authorities. The article was featured on the *Top Gear* website.

Read the article, then complete Activity 14 on page 76.

Boiling the Frog

Ever tried to boil a frog? Before hundreds of frog-loving luvvies write in, I'd like to point out that I can't claim direct experience either. Yet. But apparently,
5 all you have to do is heat the water by one degree at a time, really s-l-o-w-l-y, and before your little greenfly-munching friend knows it, he's frog soup.

   You, my fellow drivers, are just like that frog. You're up to your neck in
10 the soup pot with the flames on 'high' and you haven't noticed yet. You don't even know it, but soon you'll be driver soup and it'll be too late to do anything about it.

   Before you start thinking I'm a cylinder short of the full six, let me explain. It starts like this – let's take parking controls as an example. You used to be
15 able to park where you liked. Then suddenly a few notices spring up telling you ten minutes is your maximum. Next, because a few people are (according to the brown-nylon trousered intellectuals at the council) 'abusing' the system they arbitrarily created, there'll be wardens to check up on you and slap your legs if you take eleven minutes. Next, it's 'Pay and Display' machines and an
20 army of privatised goblins waiting, ticket-books poised.

The further step is one we've just had here in Poxford, where you have to type your car's registration number into the ticket machine to stop you giving your part-used ticket to someone else. Yes, that's right – to stop you doing what any decent human being does – being neighbourly. You've paid
25 for the space already, so why the hell should the council get someone else to pay for it too? Did you know that some councils already make more from parking than from council tax? But I forgot. We're in the Councilworld here, where every last penny must be screwed from drivers and spent on … well, what exactly? Oh yeah, more speed bumps.
30 Last year, Durham started taxing drivers for daring to drive in the city centre. Now dare to take your car into London and they will have a fiver out of your wallet to fund more speed cameras. Yet another load of friendly police forces have just signed up to keeping the cash from their cameras. Get the idea yet? The heat's being turned up on drivers.
35 What's the answer? If you want to keep your car keys you need to do something NOW. Get writing. Write to your local council, your MP, the local paper. Tell them how you need your car, how speed doesn't kill, how cars mean freedom and buses are rubbish. If you can't be bothered, don't blame me when petrol is £3 a litre, your car's got a speed limiter and parking
40 needs a second mortgage. We need a cure for anti-car claptrap.

The Spin Doctor

Activity 14

This activity will focus on the way content is used to influence the reader.

1. The article begins with a comparison. It suggests that drivers are like frogs that are being boiled slowly: soon they will be 'driver soup'. However, the writer then says 'it'll be too late to do anything about it'. What is the writer's intention here?
2. The writer then uses an example to illustrate the general point being made about drivers being 'boiled' so slowly that they don't even notice it. What example is used? Explain its effect carefully.
3. The fourth paragraph (beginning 'The further step is one we've just had here in Poxford …') deliberately tries to make us feel angry about the way councils operate. Find five 'facts' the writer has included to make us feel angry.
4. In the final two paragraphs, the writer gives three examples of what is happening to drivers. What are they?
5. The writer also gives three examples of what may happen if we do nothing. What are they?

You can see that marks can be gained relatively easily if you can identify and comment on the relevant content of any article.

Language

The selection of content is part of a writer's technique, but it is important to look at the use of language too. This involves not just finding key words and phrases, but also thinking about their purpose and effect.

The extract below is from an article about a boxing match in which a young fighter called Spencer Oliver was badly injured.

Within seconds of Oliver's triumphal ring entrance, the signs were catastrophic.

Oliver was decked with a wild hook which caught him flush on the chin. He hauled himself off the canvas but looked groggy and

5 spent. Referee Alfred Azaro looked into his eyes and allowed the fight to continue.

The 3000 crowd in the half-full Royal Albert Hall tried to raise Oliver's spirits by continually chanting his name.

10 Many of these knowledgeable fans would have witnessed the chill that went through the London Arena three years ago during Nigel Benn's fight with the American Gerald McClennan.

In an awful twist, the referee on that

15 terrible night was also Azaro, who stood in the ring aghast as McClennan was stretchered out and ended up with permanent brain damage.

Oliver tried to respond, but Devakov

20 rained in blows which the usually fleet-of-foot Oliver failed to dodge. Devakov stunned him with a punishing shot to the temple.

As the tenth round began, Oliver

25 looked weak and drained. The warning signs were there, and when a stunning right hook exploded onto his chin the audience rose in shock.

Oliver, his gumshield dropping to the floor, looked

30 up at referee Azaro with an expression which was utterly terrible. It was that of a scared young child seeking solace. He held out his hands pleading for help and then fell in a crumple to the canvas. The crowd watched in horror as he lay unconscious in the ring.

You would certainly have things to say about the content of this writing, but language is important too in creating the sense of horror.

Activity 15

The impressions the reader gets from this article are:
- Oliver is taking a lot of punches
- the punches are very powerful
- they are having a dreadful impact on him.

1. Make a list of the words that are creating these effects.
2. Time is short in exams, so pick out **four** words that you think are particularly effective. Why are these more effective?

Structure

This is how a text is organised or put together. Sometimes it is important to look at the steps in an argument to see the underlying structure. You are really just looking at the order in which the content of the text has been assembled.

How an argument can be structured

The OXFAM advertisement on page 79 is obviously very emotional. It was intended to influence readers into helping to end poverty, mainly by giving money every month. The headline and the picture play a significant part in the leaflet and you would want to say something about them. The content and language are also very powerful and the tone is conversational and polite, trying to engage the reader directly as an individual.

Read this leaflet and the numbered key on page 80. You will see how the way the text is put together helps Oxfam get its message across.

Examiner tip

Structure
If you follow the structure of a text, identifying the 'steps' in the argument, you can look for other features as you go. For example, at the end you would pick up the polite use of 'please' as an example of how tone is used to appeal to our better nature.

I can see my money saving lives. That's why 'I'm In'

❶ We're pretty lucky, aren't we? Our children will get an education. We have plenty to **❷** eat and drink. And that £8 in our pocket? Well, we'll probably use it to buy a CD or something.

❸ But for millions of people living in extreme poverty around the world, it's a very different story. That £8, for example, could **❹** be the difference between living and dying. You can help end poverty by saying 'I'm In'.

What it means to say 'I'm In'.

❺ Saying 'I'm In' is a powerful statement. It means you've chosen to join a movement of people who believe that poverty is a moral injustice and can be overcome. You can give money, volunteer your time, campaign for change, put pressure on world leaders, or simply offer your name as a sign of support. Being 'in' is your way of saying enough is enough to poverty. Right now, we're asking for money. Whatever suits your wallet. Let's see what your monthly gift could achieve:

❻
- **£8 could buy a mosquito net, which protects a family from malaria.**
- **£18 could provide safe drinking water for 25 people.**
- **£30 could build a toilet, which prevents the spread of diseases like cholera and diarrhoea.**
- **£46 could train a midwife, to safely deliver babies.**

Progress is being made. Be part of it.

The past year has seen real improvements. **❼** In April this year, for example, the government of Zambia introduced free health care for people living in rural areas. Those who couldn't afford medical help can now come forward for vital treatment. It happened because of people giving their voices in support of ending poverty. We'd like you to build on this success by saying 'I'm In'.

Please give what you can.

It's your way of saying 'I'm In'. **❽** Complete and return the attached form or call 0870 410 5025.

Visit www.oxfam.org.uk/in

How the Oxfam advert is structured

The key below refers to the leaflet on page 79. It explains how the leaflet is structured, or put together, to get the argument across.

1 The text begins by suggesting that we are very lucky.

2 Oxfam give specific examples of how we are lucky. For example, it reminds us that we have enough to eat and drink and our children get an education. It also suggests that we have money to spend on luxuries and entertainment such as CDs.

3 The text then contrasts our comfortable lifestyle with the 'extreme poverty' endured by 'millions' of people around the world.

4 Oxfam then make it clear that the £8 which we might spend on something like a CD could be the difference between life and death.

5 The next move is to claim that 'you' can help to end poverty by saying 'I'm in'. It insists that poverty is a 'moral injustice' and gives a number of ways in which we can help.

6 It lists what can be achieved by relatively small amounts of money, using bullet points to get the message across clearly and simply.

7 It tries to show that progress has been made and quotes a specific example in Zambia. It wants us to feel that we really can make a difference.

8 The advert ends with an appeal and clear directions about how to get involved.

Activity 16

Having learned how the Oxfam piece is put together, remind yourself of the 'Boiling the Frog' article (on pages 75–76). Identify the steps of the argument that the writer uses in the article. You could use bullet points to do this and you might like to work in pairs.

Tone

This is the way something is said or written, or the manner in which the reader is addressed. Writers adopt various tones, just as we do in speech, depending on whom they are addressing and what they are trying to achieve. Most of us learn at an early age how to use tone to try to get what we want!

Think about the question 'Please can I have ...?' How exactly would you say this? Your answer means that you are beginning to understand tone.

Similarly, if you fall off your chair in class, the teacher may say: 'Well, that was clever.' The meaning is the exact opposite of the literal meaning of the words, and it is achieved entirely through tone. In this case it is sarcastic, as you no doubt realised.

When you are reading, think about the tone the writer adopts, and the reason for it. There are various possibilities, but often there is a contrast between texts that are trying to seem factual, balanced and reasonable, and those that are emotional or expressing strong feelings. Some writers want to take the emotional heat out of an issue (usually if they are on the defensive or feel they are working against popular opinion), whereas others seek to gain as much emotional impact as possible. Occasionally these will be deliberately outrageous and fiercely one-sided, making no attempt to be balanced or rational.

Sometimes the tone is informal, conversational, even colloquial, and this is all part of building an image. It is also part of appealing to and engaging an audience. Direct address is personal and establishes contact with the reader. Direct or rhetorical questions can be used to challenge readers and make them think about their views and attitudes.

Below are some words you could use to describe a writer's tone. You could learn some of these so that you have a bank of words to use in the exam.

calm	aggressive	measured	ranting
serious	ironic/sarcastic	reasonable	emotional
factual	opinionated	formal	informal
earnest	elevated	flippant/lighthearted	
conversational/colloquial			

Activity 17

Re-read the article 'Boiling the Frog' on pages 75–76.

1. Which words from the list above best describe the tone of the article?
2. Find some examples to illustrate what you mean.

Headlines and titles

All headlines and titles try to 'catch the eye' or 'grab the attention', so you will get little or no credit given if that is all you say in an exam answer. It is true that headlines are used to draw the reader in, but you must describe *how* a particular headline or title makes its impact. You should be making points that apply *only* to the *particular* headline you are referring to. You need to think about its intended effect on the reader. Ask yourself: Why this headline? What is it achieving? How?

Headlines are often used to clearly introduce a topic, but sometimes they withhold information in an attempt to intrigue, or even mislead, the reader.

Some common features of headlines and titles are:
- direct address (the use of 'you' to engage the reader as an individual)
- questions (sometimes rhetorical but often direct)
- sensational, dramatic or emotive language for impact
- play on words (often witty: puns, alliteration, rhyme, etc).

Examiner tip

Avoid saying 'it makes you want to read on'. The effect of a headline can be better described using words such as 'provocative', 'arresting', 'challenging', 'intriguing', 'tasteless', 'funny' or 'sensational'.

Activity 18

Look at these headlines.

A bit of Rootail therapy

And so to bed

We're all going bananas

Rubbish attitudes laying waste to our landscape

What do you think each of these articles is about?

Activity 19

In pairs or on your own, try to explain what these headlines are about and why they are effective.

Catch us if you can chant the red devils

Political flyweight knocked out by Blair's heavyweight successor

Can you grimm and bear it?

Boys in the hoods

Don't worry if you can't think of anything useful to say about a particular headline. If you do comment on it, say something specific and precise. You will get no marks for simply saying that a headline is 'big and bold and makes you want to read on'.

Pictures

Visual images convey obvious and less obvious messages. It is usually helpful to think about a picture in relation to the text it accompanies. A picture can illustrate and/or reinforce a message. It can give reality and individuality to someone or something.

A picture may be intended to shock, to attract, or to arouse emotion. Always try to analyse the intention and the effect of pictures in texts; it is not enough to notice the existence of a picture, and simply saying what is in the picture does not help much. Some articles have more than one picture, and you should consider all of them in your response.

When looking at pictures, ask yourself the following.
1. Why this picture? What is its effect?
2. Is each picture giving the same message?
3. Do the pictures work together to reinforce the message of the text?
4. Do the pictures give different messages? If so, why?

Remember, a picture will usually link to the headline and the main text.

Activity 20

Take a look at this picture, then answer the questions beneath it.

Global warming – government told to act now

1. Why this picture? What is its effect?
2. Does the picture reinforce the message of the headline? If so, why?
3. Does the picture give a different message from the headline? If so, why?

Presentation

This is not usually a major or decisive factor in the persuasive impact of a text. Occasionally there is something useful to say, but don't get sidetracked. Look for:

- use of bold type or colour
- layout of text (bullets, fonts, text boxes)
- logos.

And always ask: What is the point or the effect of this?

For example, some techniques are used to highlight particular features, and the purpose of a logo is to encourage 'recognition' and give credibility.

Activity 21

Working in pairs, identify as many of these logos as you can. For each one, answer the following questions.

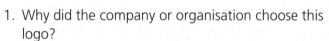

1. Why did the company or organisation choose this logo?
2. What does the logo suggest to you?
3. Do you think it is an effective logo? Why?/Why not?

Comments on presentation should not dominate your answers. The appearance and presentation of a text may attract your attention or catch your interest, but that is only the first part of the job. The really important part is **persuading**. Nobody is likely to be persuaded by a text simply because of its layout.

Putting together the persuasive techniques

Now it's time to put together all you have learnt about persuasive techniques.

Activity 22

1. You are trying to persuade a friend to accept your views on a subject you feel strongly about. Write a piece of about a page in length.

   You could write about a controversial subject such as animal rights or the environment, or about a local issue such as a school or hospital closing down. Remember the checklist:
   - approach
   - content
   - language
   - structure
   - tone
   - headlines and titles
   - pictures
   - presentation.

   You may not be able to use all of these, but you must think about the choices you make when you write.

2. Now try to identify the methods you have used, for example:
   - Did you use any statistics or figures?
   - What tone were you trying to use?

Examiner tip

Using the checklist as a framework
The best method for handling a whole text is to take it in sequence and use the checklist as a framework. Pick up points about content, language, tone and so on as they occur.

Now read the following article.

Banana campaign sheet
The latest information and ideas for action

Bananas are the UK's most popular fruit and the most valuable food product sold in British supermarkets. Yet banana farmers and workers around the world face extremely difficult and often dangerous working conditions. Bananas carrying the Fairtrade Mark are now available in Britain. This mark guarantees that the producers have had a better deal.

Cheap and cheerful?

Bananas may be cheap and popular with the consumer, but they are cheap partly because of the conditions under which they are grown. Large companies control the plantations in Latin America where the cheapest bananas are produced, but the social and environmental costs of achieving high levels of productivity are huge. The over-use of agricultural chemicals damages the environment and the health of the people exposed to them. Some 20% of the male banana workers in Costa Rica have been left sterile after handling toxic chemicals, while women in packing plants suffer double the national rate of leukaemia.

As well as being forced to endure appalling working conditions, plantation workers are also paid very poor wages. Some farmers are getting very low prices for their bananas. These can be as low as $2 for a 40lb box (3 pence per pound) – which does not even cover the cost of production. The result is that many poor farmers are losing money, and as a result are gradually losing their livelihoods.

Fairtrade bananas are packaged with the Fairtrade label and this guarantees producers are paid a fair price for their goods. Many shoppers are willing to buy Fairtrade bananas even though they cost a bit more. Over a third of the EU population said they would be prepared to pay a little more for a Fairtrade product. More than 70% of UK shoppers say they care about the conditions endured by the people who produce goods for them to consume.

Look for the Fairtrade Mark if you want to be sure the producers get a fair deal.

Supermarket action

In order for producers to benefit from Fairtrade it is crucial that Fairtrade bananas sell well. They are available in most Sainsbury's and Co-op supermarkets and early indications are that sales have been very good. However, some of the other supermarkets are currently considering whether to stock them too. The more widely available Fairtrade bananas are, the more people are likely to buy them, and the more producers will benefit - so please let your supermarket know that their customers want to buy Fairtrade!

What can you do to support Fairtrade?

If a supermarket in your area stocks Fairtrade bananas:

- Publicise Fairtrade bananas - tell friends about them.
- Buy Fairtrade bananas regularly, otherwise they will rot on supermarket shelves and will soon be dropped by the supermarket.
- Tell people to look for the Fairtrade Mark, and let them know what it stands for.

If your local store hasn't already got Fairtrade bananas:

- Please ask for them! Customer comment cards and suggestion books are read carefully by managers, and do influence decisions. Alternatively, ask the Customer Services Desk when they will have them, and leave your address so that they can get their head office's response to you.
- Get others to do the same. Supermarkets like to meet their customers' demands.

Thank You!

Live the difference - buy Fairtrade products

This table shows some of the points you might make if you were planning an answer to the question below. However, you would not have time to make notes of this sort in the exam.

How does the Fairtrade campaign sheet try to persuade you to buy only Fairtrade bananas? **(10)**

Content	Tells us bananas are popular
	Mentions 'difficult and often dangerous' working conditions
	Tells us Fairtrade bananas are available in the UK
	Tells us several times that Fairtrade 'guarantees' a fair price or a better deal for producers
	Mentions damage caused to environment
	Mentions health problems suffered by workers (uses specific examples)
	Bananas are cheap but only because producers get low prices and workers get low wages
	Uses statistic to make the point (3p per pound)
	Tells us 70 per cent of UK shoppers say they care about how workers are treated
	Suggests one-third of EU population are prepared to pay more
	Argues that if we buy Fairtrade, more supermarkets will stock them
	Tells us exactly what to do
Language	'appalling' – suggests conditions are dreadful/horrible
	'a bit more' and 'a little more' try to suggest that we will only have to make a small sacrifice/pay just a little extra
Tone	Polite (uses 'please' and 'thank you')
	Uses commands (imperatives)
	Uses 'you' to involve the reader directly
Structure	Starts with the terrible conditions and wages
	Tells you how you can help
	Describes the problem and then gives the solution
Presentation	Uses logo for recognition and to give credibility
	Bullet points give simple, clear instructions
	Uses questions to make us think about the issues
Approach	Appeals to our better nature
	Tries to make us feel guilty
	Tries to make us feel sympathy for workers and farmers
	Wants us to pay more to help others
	Makes us feel we can really make a difference
Pictures	None
Headlines	Nothing to say

Activity 23

The planning in the table on page 88 is very thorough. You are unlikely to produce this much in the 10–15 minutes you should spend answering this question in the exam. So, you need to be able to identify the key points that relate to the question:

How does the Fairtrade campaign sheet try to persuade you to buy only Fairtrade bananas? **(10)**

1. Working in pairs, using the table on page 88 or your own ideas, write down the main points you think your answer should include.
2. On your own, in no more than 15 minutes, write an answer to the question above.

Comparison and evaluation of texts

What will I learn?

In this unit I will:
- learn to compare and contrast two texts
- learn how to evaluate two texts
- look at the ways in which this type of question can be asked
- analyse answers from other students
- practise answering this type of question.

You are required to answer a question in Section A of Paper 2 (it is usually A4) that involves looking at two texts. This is known as 'cross referencing'.

The wording of the question varies from year to year, but basically there are two ways of testing your ability to 'cross reference'.

'Comparing and contrasting' questions

The first is to ask you to compare and contrast the two texts. This means you are looking for specific similarities and differences, and your personal views and opinions are not required. You will waste time and get no marks if you ignore the question and simply give your views about the texts or the issues they discuss.

These questions are worded like this.
- These two texts give very different impressions. In what ways are they different?
- Compare and contrast what these two texts tell you about …
- These two texts are about … Compare and contrast them using the following headings …

'Evaluating' questions

The second type of question asks you to evaluate the texts. This means saying which you prefer, or commenting on strengths and weaknesses.

This is your opportunity to say what you think about the texts, although you must remember that you are discussing their strengths and weaknesses. The texts are often about controversial issues and you must resist the temptation to launch into a rant. You should concentrate on discussing the texts. Your views on their subject matter should not distract you.

The idea is to express a preference and justify it by examining the details of the two texts. There is no 'right answer' here: you are free to prefer either text. The examiner will look at the quality of your analysis and the evidence on which your preference is based.

These questions are worded like this.
- Which of these two texts do you find more effective, and why?
- Which aspects of these two texts do you find most influential?
- Which of these texts do you find more convincing, and why?
- Using information from both texts, explain what/why/how far …

In both types of question you will often be given a list of bullet points to follow, which you should use to give structure to your answer. If you are told to organise your answer into paragraphs using the bullet points as headings, then you should do exactly that. Remember that the examiner is trying to help you and you should take whatever help is offered.

To help you with the first type of question (comparing and contrasting), read the following texts and complete the activity that follows.

Remember

The first type of question does not involve your opinions; you should stay out of the argument. The second type of question does ask what you think, but it asks how effective you think the texts are, not what you think about the issue.

Going the distance

At this year's London marathon, Fauja Singh aims to beat his best time of six hours. It seems a modest ambition – but then, he is 93. Anne Johnson finds out what drives him.

He maintains a steady, moderate pace like a man entirely in control of himself and his destiny. He likes routine and he runs nine or 10 miles a day, every day, clocking up 70 miles a week. There is nothing particularly unusual about that, you think – there are plenty of people who take their training seriously – until you discover that this man is 93 years old.

Still more surprisingly, Fauja Singh hasn't been running for very long. He took it up when his wife died 11 years ago and, since then, it has been the main focus in his life. […]

In all, he has done six marathons – four in London and one each in Toronto and New York. When he runs in London on April 18, he is hoping to come in below the six-hour mark – having crossed the finishing line last year in six hours, two minutes and 43 seconds. […]

Fauja is intensely competitive and loves the fact that he has beaten the London marathon record for his age group – runners in their 90s – every year. […]

Fauja's desire to win and set records is the driving force in his running. This year's London marathon will probably be the last he runs on an annual basis and he says he wants to go out on a high. The idea of finishing a marathon with thousands of younger people behind him is clearly an alluring one and, ultimately, what keeps him going.

Fauja's other passion, alongside running and the desire to compete, is his Sikh belief that a person has to work and share the fruits of his labours with others. Currently, he runs for Bliss, a charity that helps premature babies; he sometimes also runs under the banner of the British Heart Foundation in honour of some of his jogging friends who have taken up running, several in marathons, since heart attacks. […]

He looks the picture of health. When I saw him, he ran several laps of his pavement circuit – exactly 2.147 km – at 15 minutes each and with no rest in between other than a few swigs from a bottle of water waiting for him on a wall. He was not even breathless.

He weighs just eight stone which, for his height of six feet, is almost nothing. He eats a basic vegetarian Punjabi diet, doesn't drink or smoke, and avoids new foods in case they upset his system.

A simple man of few desires, Fauja says he is grateful to God for giving him the opportunity and the talent to do what he does. He meditates every morning before training and prays every day, morning and evening. But can so much strenuous exercise be sensible at his age? […]

The world record for the oldest person to run a marathon is 98, and Fauja would dearly like to beat that. So he is hoping to make a one-off comeback in the 2009 London marathon.

Not many weeks later in the London Marathon I ran the best race I had ever run in my life, or ever will.

It is, for anyone, a nervy feeling, pacing Blackheath too early on a cold Sunday morning, seeing the crowds and yet blind to them, hearing the loudspeakers and yet somehow miles
5 away, wondering why you ever entered and – worse – why you ever told everyone you were entering. […]

Then the cannon, and you're off. Wave at the cameras, just in case. It's a human traffic jam. Why didn't I cheat more? Then the road clears and – hey – this is OK! What's wrong? Why am I going so fast? Surely I can't keep this up? Look – somebody's recognised me – they're all
10 waving and cheering … a frenzy of applause – surely I can't be that famous? I'm not. It's Jimmy Savile in a gold lamé tracksuit, in front. […]

How, I groaned to myself, had I even thought I could carry this off? Obviously I was too old. At thirty-six I should have bowed out with dignity the previous year … all that training wasted … thousands of miles … 2 a.m. sessions down the Wandsworth Road after a late sitting
15 in Parliament … the policeman who thought I was a midnight smash-and-grab raider until I showed him my MP.'s pass. I waved wearily at the many people who didn't know me in E.14.

They cheered back, a huge cheer. And a band was playing. And that stitch – where was it? Gone. Disappeared while my mind was off it. I sped up a bit and checked the time. If I could only keep this up … No, I said, stop thinking about it. Just run. My pace quickened after that.
20 People in front of me were wobbling into the arms of spectators. Good, I thought. Let them.

They say the marathon's a friendly race: 'all in it together', they say. Together? Can there be any other occasion when so many thousands gather to do the same thing, in the same place at the same time, yet each entirely alone, each in his or her own world, each with so different an idea of why he or she is there? Each conscious of a sympathetic fellow-feeling for
25 every other runner in trouble … and yet – he's fading, I'm still here; one down, ten thousand to go. Hah. […]

The miles around the Isle of Dogs melted and I was feeling fine. The carbohydrate-loaded diet really did work. All that stuff about 'hitting the wall' at eighteen miles was just old wives' tales, I told myself powering past the nineteen-mile marker. […]
30 Then the wall did hit me. It was awful. People around me began dropping like flies, and all at once I sympathised and knew what they were going through. I too was ready to drop. Narrow Street passed in a grim haze. Five miles left – could I keep any kind of a pace going?. I slackened speed but ground on. This really hurt. […]

Big Ben at last. The last mile had been torture. […]
35 2.32.55–2.32.56 … And I came in at 2.32.57: fastest MP ever, again, and 385th out of 20,000. […]

But what a feeling, inside. I resolved never to enter another London Marathon. This result was so much better than I had expected, so much better than I deserved. Not for me the slow decline as year succeeds year and you enter the veterans' section and begin comparing
40 yourself not with the generality but with fellow-members of a sub-group you redefine every year to make it small enough to hold your head up in. Then at sixty the knee troubles hit. No, I resolved, this is the best I'll ever do so I'll quit while I'm ahead; and I did.

Matthew Parris

Activity 24

Fauja Singh and Matthew Parris are both marathon runners. To help you compare the two men, copy and complete the table below by finding evidence in the texts on pages 91 and 92. Notice that some of this information is simply factual, so you should be able to find these points quickly.

	Fauja Singh	Matthew Parris
Their ages		
Their diet		
Their fastest marathon times		
Their attitude towards the other runners		
Their attitude to running marathons in the future		

Read the two texts, an extract and an old leaflet for the Big Pit mine, that follow. Then complete the comparison activity on page 96, which follows after some guidance.

The following non-fiction extract is taken from *The Road to Wigan Pier* which was first published in 1937 after the author, George Orwell, had visited the industrial north of England. Here he is describing what it is like in a working coal mine.

The time to go there is when the machines are roaring and the air is black with coal dust, and when you can actually see what the miners have to do. At those times the place is like hell, or at any rate like my own mental picture of hell. Most of the things one imagines in hell are there – heat, noise, confusion, darkness, foul air, and, above
5 all, unbearably cramped space. Everything except the fire, for there is no fire down there except the feeble beams of lamps and electric torches which scarcely penetrate the clouds of coal dust.

When you have finally got there – and getting there is a job in itself […] you crawl through the last line of pit props and see opposite you a shiny black wall three or four
10 feet high. This is the coal face. Overhead is the smooth ceiling made by the rock from which the coal has been cut; underneath is the rock again, so that the gallery you are in is only as high as the ledge of coal itself, probably not much more than a yard. The first impression of all, overmastering everything else for a while, is the frightful, deafening din from the conveyor belt which carries the coal away. You cannot see very far,
15 because the fog of coal dust throws back the beam of your lamp, but you can see on either side of you the line of half-naked kneeling men, one to every four or five yards, driving their shovels under the fallen coal and flinging it swiftly over their left shoulders. They are feeding it on to the conveyor belt, a moving rubber belt a couple of feet wide which runs a yard or two behind them. Down this belt a glittering river of coal races
20 constantly. In a big mine it is carrying away several tons of coal every minute.

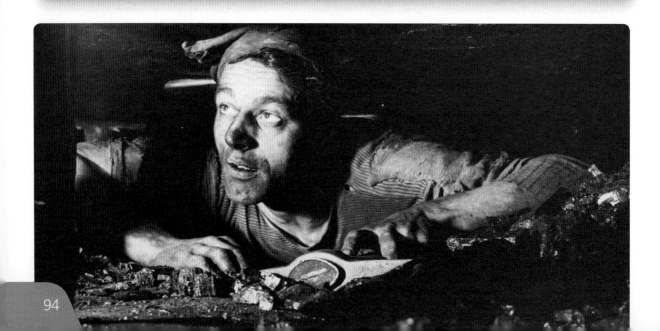

ON A HILLSIDE at the top of the Afon Lwyd Valley stands one of the last memorials to a distinguished industrial heritage.

From its pithead baths you can see at a glance how the iron and coal industries transformed the landscape of the South Wales valleys.

At Blaenafon the community and its structures are still largely intact. The 18th century ironworks; the ironmasters' houses, church and schools; the workmen's Institute, "Co-op", chapels and the town itself are living images of more than two centuries of industrial history. Coal is still mined here, in levels on the hillside and by opencast on the valley floor. But the reason why over a million people came from all over the world to Blaenafon during the last ten years is...

'A unique and unforgettable experience'

BIG PIT

Unique underground tours

Big Pit is a real colliery. Sunk in 1880 and incorporating much earlier coal and ironstone workings, it produced coal on a large scale until it closed in 1980. When the coal stopped coming out, the colliery simply started taking visitors in.

If you're 5 years of age or over, you too can benefit from the fascinating experience that has made Big Pit the most visited coal mine in Wales.

The miners and engineers who maintain the colliery also act as guides and are noted for their friendliness and good humour. They will lend you a helmet and cap lamp and take you down the 90 metre shaft in the pit cage to walk through underground roadways, air doors, stables and engine houses built by past generations of mineworkers. This is no mere simulation and the guide's commentary and anecdotes are based on his own experiences.

The tours take about an hour and you will need warm clothing and sensible walking footwear.

A mine of information too!

Back on the surface you can explore the colliery buildings - the winding engine-house, the blacksmiths workshop, the pithead baths and others - and learn more about the story of coal from exhibitions and simulated mining galleries.

The miners' canteen is now a licensed cafeteria and the old fitting shop is a gift shop full of books, crafts and popular souvenirs. There are picnic areas, disabled facilities and all the amenities you would expect to find in a major tourist attraction. But we have tried not to let all this detract from the

stark realism of a genuinely evocative site.

Come and see for yourself. You will be very welcome and we don't think you'll be disappointed.

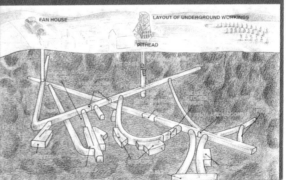

Before you tackle the activity that follows, you need to consider how the two pieces differ. If you look at the Orwell passage, there are details about a 'real' coal mine, such as:

- it is noisy
- it is dusty
- it is cramped
- it is hot
- coal is being mined
- it is a place of incredibly hard work
- it is like 'hell'.

Big Pit is clearly not a 'real' mine:

- it is no longer a working mine
- no coal is produced
- it is a museum/a memorial
- it has the usual visitor attractions (gift shop, picnic area)
- it is a 'theme park' version of a mine.

However, you could argue that in some ways Big Pit is a 'real' mine! Can you think of any?

Activity 25

You now have the information on which to base an answer, but it still needs to be organised into a convincing response. Using the information you have been given, write your answer to the question below in no more than 15 minutes:

The leaflet claims that a visit to 'Big Pit' is a visit to a 'real' coal mine. Using information from both the extract and the leaflet (on pages 94 and 95), explain how far you think this is true.

What have I learnt?

In this section we covered:

- how to select relevant details from a passage and present them clearly
- how texts attempt to present an impression or image of their subject
- how texts attempt to present a viewpoint or attitude towards their subject
- how texts target particular individuals or groups of people
- techniques used to analyse the ways in which writers try to influence readers
- how to compare, contrast and evaluate two texts
- types of Paper 2 Section A exam questions

How confident do you now feel about each of the above? You could note down the points you feel confident about and those that you need to go back to.

Introduction

What will Section B of Paper 1 look like?

In Paper 1 Section B you will have to produce two pieces of writing.

You will have to write to inform, explain or describe; and to explore, imagine or entertain. The exam paper tests these skills by requiring you to produce:

- a piece of descriptive writing
- a piece of narrative/personal writing.

They are different types of writing. This section will try to explain what the differences are and how you can improve your performance in both tasks.

What will the questions be like?

- Question B1 is the descriptive piece. You will not have a choice of title.
- Question B2 is the narrative/personal writing. There are four different types of title in the choice of five tasks that you will have to choose from in the exam.

What should I do?

You will have one hour to complete this section, so you need to think quickly and be careful about how you use the time. B1 must not take up more than 25 minutes. You must leave **at least** 40 minutes for B2. The examiner who marks your work will assess your writing in terms of:

- content and organisation
- technical accuracy in spelling, punctuation and grammar.

This means you have to work quickly, but you must take care to write as accurately as you can. This section of the book will help you to get organised.

Paper 1 Section B sample question

Here is a selection of typical writing tasks for this section of the exam.

B1 questions

- Describe the scene at a fairground on a winter's night.
- Describe the scene during your morning break – at school, at college, at work or at home.
- A local newspaper is running a weekly feature about local 'characters'. It describes people who are well known in your local community. You decide to contribute to this series by writing about one or two 'characters'. Write your article.
- Write a description of a market at a busy time.
- Describe the people in the queue at a checkout in a supermarket.
- Describe the scene in a dining hall or canteen at lunchtime.
- Describe the scene at a busy tourist attraction. You could describe a theme park, a museum, a zoo or a historic site. However, you are free to use your own ideas.
- Describe the scene on a beach or in a park on a summer's day.
- Describe the scene at **one** of the following: a train station; a bus station; a ferry terminal; an airport.
- Describe the scene in a large clothing store on the first day of the January sales.
- Describe the scene in your school or college on a day when it has snowed heavily.

> **Remember**
>
> Always ask yourself: Who would I see here and what would they be doing? In exam conditions, you would have about 25 minutes to write about a page.

B2 questions

- The Gamble
- Write a story that ends with the words: '… and it just showed that you can't always get what you want.'
- Write about a time when you showed courage.
- The Betrayal
- Continue the story: 'The relentless icy wind buffeted his whole body as he staggered on …'

Descriptive writing

What makes good descriptive writing?

In Section B of Paper 1 your first task is to write a descriptive piece. In this type of writing you are trying to use words to paint a picture for the reader. There are only three possible topics for descriptive writing in Section B of Paper 1: **places**, **events** and **people**.

In descriptive writing, the writer should be positioned as an observer. One approach is to act like a fixed camera, recording what is seen and heard, and perhaps using the other senses too. For example, you could be sitting in a stadium, recording what is going on in a sporting event, or at the checkout in a supermarket, observing what is happening around you.

Another approach is to move around a particular location like a moving camera. For example, you could be moving through a funfair or a market, trying to convey the sights, sounds and atmosphere. Remember that a camera can zoom in close to look at specific details and individuals.

Describing the scene at a bus station is not the same as writing 'The day I caught a bus'. It is important that you write a piece of description rather than a narrative. A narrative tells a story, while description paints a picture using words. The pages that follow will explain the techniques you should use in your descriptive writing and look at each of them in more detail.

Write in sentences

You have to organise your writing into sentences, and examiners will be looking to see if you have control of sentence construction. Sentences must have at least one main verb; descriptive writing without main verbs is not as effective. A main verb shows the time when an action takes place: present, past or future.

You can use the present tense in one of two ways (the main verbs are underlined in the examples below).

1. She <u>walks</u> or 2. She <u>is walking</u>.

If you used the past tense you would say:

1. She <u>walked</u> or 2. She <u>was walking</u>.

Below are some 'sentences' from a piece of work that was produced in exam conditions. The student is describing a group of schoolchildren.

> The children all talking, waiting patiently, like a rainbow in all their different coats.
> The girls all standing waiting with hair bands and flower bobbles.
> The boys wrestling or reminiscing over their 1–0 win on the playground at breaktime.

None of these is really a sentence, because none of them has a main verb, but it is easy to make them into sentences (the examples below are in the past tense).

> The children **were** all talking, waiting patiently, like a rainbow in all their different coats.
> The girls **were** all standing waiting with hair bands and flower bobbles.
> The boys **were** wrestling or reminiscing over their 1–0 win on the playground at breaktime.

Examiner tip

Write at least one side
The instructions on the exam paper suggest that you should write 'about a page'. Don't write half a page, as the examiner may feel that you haven't done the job properly. However, you don't have time to write a lot more than a page. If you have particularly large or small handwriting, you may need to adjust the length of your answer.

Remember

Exam timing
You have about 20–25 minutes for Question B1.

The words in bold are called auxiliary verbs; they are needed to show the tense of the verbs. However, what really matters is that you know how and when to use them.

You could also use the simple past tense:

> The children all **talked**, waiting patiently, like a rainbow in all their different coats.
>
> The girls all **stood** waiting with hair bands and flower bobbles.
>
> The boys **wrestled** or **reminisced** over their 1–0 win on the playground at breaktime.

Activity 1

The 'sentences' in the paragraph below also have no main verbs. Re-write this paragraph putting the sentences in the present tense. For example: To my left **are sitting** a young couple, anxiously feeding their toddler chicken nuggets dipped in tomato sauce.

To my left sitting a young couple, anxiously feeding their toddler chicken nuggets dipped in tomato sauce. The two-year-old crying and whining, putting his hands up to his mouth as if to say 'No, no more'. The group of young people to my right laughing, shouting and flirting. One of the boys stealing a girl's milkshake and she leaning across her friends, giggling happily, to try and snatch it back. I can hear a radio playing faintly. The newest, noisiest dance track struggling to be heard in the room full of people, resembling a school canteen.

Organise your work into paragraphs

It is important to organise your writing into paragraphs. A page of writing should probably have between three and six paragraphs. If there are too few, your writing will be simply a 'chunk' and quite difficult to read. If there are too many, it will look 'scrappy' and nothing will be developed in any detail.

Pay attention to adverbs and adjectives

The point of descriptive writing is to create a vivid mental picture to give your readers as clear a sense as possible of a place, an event or a person.

Adverbs are the words that describe verbs and tell us how an action is performed. For example, you could say that someone 'walked' across a room, but if you add the adverb 'casually', you will give a more precise image of someone walking in an unhurried way. The adverb 'briskly' would change this image completely and show a sense of urgency.

Adjectives describe nouns and tell us what they look like. For example, think about the mental image you get from the sentence below:

'In the corner there was a couple holding hands.'

Now read this:

'In the corner there was an elderly couple holding hands.'

How did that change your mental picture and your response?

Always consider whether an adverb or an adjective would help to create the effect you want.

Activity 2

The piece of writing below has had all its adverbs and adjectives removed. Working in pairs, try to decide where the words listed in the box would fit best. Use a dictionary if there are words here you don't understand.

The air hung **ADVERB** thick and greasy. **ADJECTIVE** aromas both pleasant and unpleasant filled the nostrils of the observer. The **ADJECTIVE** chatter was a dull roar, the **ADJECTIVE** heat exerting pressure on the body. The queue jostled and jibed, everyone vying and straining to reach the counter where vats of **ADJECTIVE** soup, casserole or vegetables stood bubbling, the aroma of spices and tomatoes scenting the air.

Behind the counter, women in overalls and nets to cover their hair looked bored but busy, rattling off the day's food choices **ADVERB** to every second person. They doled out food with ladles, **ADVERB**, knowing the right amount to fill the bowl full, but not too full. There were cutbacks and **ADJECTIVE** portions with **ADJECTIVE** prices were the order of the day.

At the till, a **ADJECTIVE** woman with salt-and-pepper hair poking **ADVERB** out of her hairnet totted up the totals and took the money – 'that will be two pounds fifteen pence' or 'a bowl of soup makes three pounds five pence' – handing out change with **ADJECTIVE** accuracy.

The queue moved onwards, as people sat together in small groups, some in a hurry shovelling food without a thought, others **ADVERB** enjoying the meal, talking **ADVERB** among themselves.

higher	short
relentless	serenely
pleasantly	monotonously
pungent	efficiently
smaller	messily
steaming	ceaseless
faintly	stifling

Think about the verbs you use

Thinking about the verbs you use links with the points about adverbs and adjectives on page 102. Your task as a writer is to give the reader as clear and precise a picture as you can manage, and the verbs you use are an important part of this.

Read these two versions of a short extract from a piece of descriptive writing.

1.

> The mothers take a child each and escort them out of the gate into the street, one holding her child's arm behind her, and another asking what her little boy had spent the day doing.

2.

> The mothers grab a child each and frogmarch them out of the gate into the street, one yanking her child's arm behind her, and another demanding to know what her little boy had spent the day doing.

The first version paints a picture that could be seen as warm and friendly with the mothers acting pleasantly and seeming pleased to see their children.

The difference between the two extracts is that four verbs have changed in the second version. They make the action seem more aggressive and physical, suggesting that the mothers are in a hurry and in charge. For example, 'yanking' is much stronger than 'holding' and suggests more physical force. 'Demanding to know' is much more aggressive than 'asking' and the lines now communicate the mothers' impatience.

Activity 3

The verbs underlined in the five sentences below work, but could be stronger and more precise. Working in pairs, try to replace them with better words.

1. Close to the gate, one woman <u>holds</u> a newborn baby in her arms.
2. A gaggle of mothers <u>talk about</u> the nursery teacher's forthcoming marriage.
3. Echoing from every speaker is an over-excited orchestra <u>playing</u> hysterical themes for each ride.
4. Cheerful sounds, the musical equivalent of candyfloss, <u>play</u> through hidden speakers in the walls.
5. The girl <u>drinks</u> her Coke, then <u>coughs</u> as the bubbles go up her nose. Her companion, a boy her age, laughs and <u>hits</u> her on the back.

Try to write from memory rather than imagination

Sometimes you will have to describe a place or an event by relying on your imagination, or what you have seen on television or in the cinema. However, most of the time you will be asked to describe familiar things. It is always a good idea, where possible, to use your personal experience, to give your description a sense of realism.

For example, if you are asked to describe a supermarket, then picture the one you go to and try to give an image of what it is like. Making it real avoids the problem of writing something that is difficult to believe.

Another example might be to describe the scene in the waiting room of a dentist's surgery. Most people will have visited a dentist at some time, so this is an easy opportunity simply to picture the scene and start writing. You could combine your memories of two or three visits to a waiting room and pick out the most interesting characters, or just imagine people you know being there, such as a friend, relative or neighbour.

However, you must be careful not to lose your sense of reality. If you tried to suggest that the waiting room was more like a medieval torture chamber than a place where people waited for treatment, with screams and rivers of blood, this would be totally unconvincing. Ask yourself: Have I ever actually heard anyone screaming while sitting in a dentist's waiting room? The answer is almost certainly 'No.'

Activity 4

It is helpful to use the senses in descriptive writing. Touch and taste are sometimes relevant, but sights, sounds and smells really do add to the picture you are trying to create.

Make a list of:
- what you would see in the waiting room of a dentist's surgery
- what you would hear in the waiting room of a dentist's surgery
- what you would smell in the waiting room of a dentist's surgery.

Be as specific and precise as you can.

Make it sound real

Try to include authentic details, including physical description and snatches of dialogue. This is what you would actually see and hear in a particular situation.

This is simply a way of making a scene seem real and convincing. For example, in the dentist's waiting room you would find the old magazines, or the tank full of fish or the posters about dental health, but the physical details would be different if you were describing a classroom in a school or a corner shop.

Snatches of dialogue can make the scene more lively, and they are a good way of showing character, as in the short extract below.

Behind me two tiny children are rummaging in the toy box. A gasp of delight is quickly followed by 'Oh, yes! They've got Buzz Lightyear!'

The reception door opens and a cheerful pink-lipped
5 woman sticks her head around the door.

'Mr James?' she trills, smiling. 'Just a word if you please.'

A young man in school uniform stands up hesitantly and walks across the room. His discomfort is apparently
10 magnified in a blazer that appears two sizes too big for him and trousers with a distinct crease down the front.

'Nothing to worry about love, just routine,' the nurse reassures him soothingly, noticing the pained apprehension on his face.

The words of the children show their delight and excitement without any need for additional explanation, and the character of the nurse emerges very clearly in the way she speaks to the young man. Dialogue is a useful device, but don't overdo it.

Describe but do not tell a story

This is a very important point and one that must be followed. This task is not intended to be a short story, and you should not spend time on the journey to the supermarket or the dentist's surgery, or what you had for breakfast or what you did when you got home or any other irrelevant material.

Avoid writing in the first person

For example, in the extract below a student is describing a festival of punk music, but does not use 'I' at all or make any personal references.

> Punkfest took place in a dark, square room, a metal stage at one side supporting five angry musicians and a variety of instruments. The singer clung to the microphone while shouting incomprehensible lyrics, his eyes screwed up tightly. The drummer seemed bored by the whole thing, not even looking down as he beat away at a rhythm.

This is a good way of avoiding a narrative approach – you should be the camera, not the leading man or woman, in this drama.

Some writers use the second person (*you*) and do it successfully. However, the third person (*he*, *she*, *it* or *they*) is the safest option. It is possible to include some personal reflections or comments, but be careful to stick to description.

Remember

You are not the leading actor in this drama, so you should avoid using the first person.

Avoid generalisations

Generalised observation is not very successful for two reasons. First, it is usually unconvincing. If you are constantly writing 'People are doing this' or 'Everyone is doing that', your writing becomes boring and unrealistic. The truth is that in any given situation, everyone is not doing or thinking or saying the same thing. Second, it restricts what you can say. For example, if everyone is staring at the wall in the dentist's surgery, then what else can you say about the people who are there?

'Close-ups' can work well. Notice in the example below how the writer starts with a large group of children but 'zooms in' on one boy and the classroom assistant, and describes them in detail.

A mob of children began to appear at the door of the nursery. There was a small boy slumped against the wall of the nursery clutching the hand of the classroom assistant. He had a sprinkle of freckles across his nose, scuffed Spiderman trainers and a peeling sticker on his sweatshirt. The assistant was glancing at her manicured nails, tilting them like paddles in the sun, while keeping a firm grip of the boy's hand.

Focus on the individuals who inhabit the scene

Most scenes or situations will have people in them, unless you are asked to describe a deserted beach or an empty shop – but this is highly unlikely!

This gives you the opportunity to focus on the characters who are present, and to describe what they look like, how they are dressed, what they are doing, what they may be saying and even what they are thinking. In a relatively short piece of writing, you probably only need to focus on three or four characters.

For example, in a dentist's waiting room you might see a receptionist, a mother with a child, a teenager, an elderly man or woman and perhaps a married couple. What other characters might appear in this scene?

Always ask yourself the question: Who would I expect to see in this location? Then think about what you would expect them to be doing or saying. If you get that right, you can build your writing around the character sketches.

Use proper nouns where appropriate

Proper nouns are names of things, and always start with a capital letter. Using these is a way of adding reality to the scene. If someone is reading a magazine, it is helpful to say which magazine it is; this also helps to develop a sense of character. For example, if a young man is reading *Top Gear* magazine, the reader picks up the hint that he is interested in cars and other details about the character could flow from this. On the other hand, you might get a very different image of a young person who is reading *Viz* or *FHM* or *Cosmopolitan*.

Similarly, saying there is a poster on the wall in a medical centre is good, but it is much better to say what it says e.g. 'Teen Pregnancy – the Facts' or 'Look out for your mate'.

If you are describing a park, name it. 'The park' becomes, for example, 'Victoria Park' and the sense of realism increases, making your writing more believable. If you mention a doctor, why not give them a name? This persuades the examiner that you are really attempting to describe what you know.

Assessment of descriptive writing

Remember that the assessment of descriptive writing is under two broad headings. These are:
• content and organisation
• sentence structure, punctuation and spelling.

Two examples of descriptive writing follow, produced by students in exam conditions. They include comments from an examiner and as they cover different levels of ability they are given different grades. The task the students had to complete was:

Describe the scene at a primary or nursery school at the end of the day. **(20)**

Read the two student responses and the comments from the examiner.

Answer 1

Rather foolishly, some might say, The Three Bears Nursery
School **1** had been built on top of a steep hill, **2** the side of which
was blanketed with swirls of snowy daisies. **3**

The nursery itself was strawberry red with a white roof and
5   foundations, which from a distance made the building look like a
greedily filled jam sandwich. **4** **5**

At the foot of the hill, **6** shiny Volvo and Mercedes people **7**
were starting to arrive, backing up into regimented **8** parking
spaces. The scene resembled a lunatic's game of 'Connect Four'. **9**

10   The parents started to ascend the aptly named 'Heart Attack
Hill' **10** to retrieve their toddlers. One father **11** jokingly began
some enthusiastic leg lunges before starting the upward trek.
His face implied that his actions were in jest, but his head kept
turning sharply to his left, perhaps to ascertain whether the young
15   Scandinavian mother **12** was appreciating his impromptu display of
physical fitness. **13**

The first parents entered the nursery and soon the trickle of
infants began to stream **14** out of the red doors, many looking like
brightly coloured pom-poms in their ridiculously insulated winter
20   coats. **15**

One small girl began to run down the hill, falling over as she
went, and bouncing on her pink head before coming to a halt. The
child was thankfully intact. She got up and wailed heartily. **16** Her
father had not seen the incident, but tore **17** his gaze away from
25   the young Scandinavian mother and rushed over to comfort the
distraught pink pom-pom that was his most precious treasure. **18**

Answer 1 – examiner comments

1 The name is an amusing touch, but it also gives a sense of realism and makes it specific and individual.

2 The fact that the school is at the top of the hill is significant as the writing develops.

3 The extra information about the daisies is included to add to the mental picture. The verb 'blanketed' is the perfect choice of vocabulary.

4 This paragraph neatly describes the physical appearance of the building, using colour and a simile which is unusual and striking.

5 You get a vivid picture of the building from the comparison to a 'greedily filled jam sandwich'.

6 This points the reader to a precise place – the foot of the hill – where the parents are beginning to arrive.

7 Notice the use of proper nouns again. There is real flair here as the writer defines the people through their cars.

8 Good choice of vocabulary.

9 A witty, inventive image to reinforce the picture.

10 Another amusing touch, using proper nouns.

11 The 'zoom lens' is now used to focus on an individual character.

12 Another character appears here. What picture do you get of her?

13 Notice how the writer hints at what is going on here.

14 There is a clever use of metaphor here as the 'trickle' becomes a 'stream'.

15 The simile of the children creates a strong mental image.

16 Notice the choice of 'wailed' instead of the weaker 'cried' and how the adverb 'heartily' strengthens the impression of the child crying at considerable volume.

17 The use of the verb 'tore' to describe how difficult it is for the man to focus his attention is very effective. The relationship between the characters now comes together very neatly.

18 Organised into six clear paragraphs.

What did the examiner think?

Answer 1 The writer has clearly enjoyed describing this scene and it is an entertaining read. This piece of writing is well constructed and the vocabulary is also good. It has shape, the characters engage our interest and, above all, it keeps us reading and smiling. There are no errors in this piece of work. The sentence structures are varied and totally controlled, the punctuation is accurate and the spelling of all words, including the difficult ones, is perfect. It is this level of technical ambition and accuracy, added to the qualities in content and organisation, which make this a clear example of an A*.

Answer 2

I walked through the lane **(1)**, which was covered in an unpleasant array of an assortment of litter. **(2)** I dodged in and out of the bacteria infested litter and headed toward the hustle and bustle of the main road. My little boy, James, was coming out of his nursery, probably dying to tell me of what adventrous **(3)** mischief he had achieved this time. I ventured along the busy road, my footsteps drowned out by the rushing cars. A swift breeze blew pleasantly **(4)** at me, cooling me down as the sun beat down on my neck. **(5)**

The nursery was now visible, and I walked steadily toward it. I had arrived at the compact nursery. There was a nearby bench with a memorial plaque **(6)** that glistened in the sun. I strolled **(7)** over and took a seat. I sat there alone. I felt really solitary. I glanced at my Rolex watch. 3.21. Nine minutes of waiting. Tick followed tock. The bell eventually sounded. **(8)**

The little toddlers ran excitedly out of the door. Their little bags clenched tight in their sweaty palms. **(9)** My Jamesy had left the building and sprinted joyfully toward me. He wrapped himself around my leg like a claw. We dodged all the mothers with prams and he held my hand firmly as if he feared losing me. His little mouth never shut on the way back. He told me of his pleasant happenings during his day. He stopped to catch breath. He wiped his brow, he was dripping like a tap, full of sweat. **(10)** The main road drowned out his squeaky little voice. We headed for the lane. The assortment of litter meant James had to go on my back. **(11)** He felt special because he was so high up and he enjoyed every minute of it.

Answer 2 – examiner comments

1 Use of first-person is not a good idea, as it leads to narrative rather than description.

2 The phrasing of 'an unpleasant array of an assortment of litter' is very clumsy. It is either an array or an assortment, but not both.

3 Note the incorrect spelling of 'adventrous'.

4 A 'swift' breeze does not really fit with the adverb 'pleasantly'.

5 The writer has written quite a lot and not even reached the nursery yet!

6 – **7** Good vocabulary.

8 The use of time to structure this section is fine. The narrator is clearly the sort of person who can afford Rolex watches!

9 Not a sentence.

10 Not a sentence. Misuse of comma.

11 The obsession with litter is unconvincing. The litter must be very deep if the little boy has to be carried on her back. Perhaps they are taking a short cut through some sort of tip?

Activity 5

In pairs, using the examiner's comments above and your own ideas, summarise how effective you think Answer 2 on page 112 is. You should use the assessment headings:
- content and organisation
- sentence structure, punctuation and spelling.

Activity 6

Now, write your own piece of descriptive writing on the following topic:

Describe the scene at a primary or nursery school on a snowy morning in winter as the children are arriving.

This is a very different scene from the two examples you have just read.

Make sure your writing is realistic. The following bullets should help you.

- Write at least one side (no less but not much more).
- Write in sentences and paragraphs.
- Pay attention to adverbs and adjectives.
- Think about the verbs you use.
- Try to write from memory rather than imagination.
- Describe but do not tell a story.
- Avoid generalisations (close-ups are better).
- Focus on the individuals who inhabit the scene.
- Avoid using the first person (use the third person).
- Try to give authentic details, including physical description.
- Use proper nouns where appropriate (names of things).

Think about who would be in this scene and what they would be doing or saying. You could include details about their appearance, their clothes, their age and their gender. The weather is important in this task.

Here are a few points of focus you could use to get you started:

children	**teachers**
caretaker	**parents**
a teenage girl	**a man in a suit**
lollipop lady	**an elderly couple**

Verbs, adverbs and adjectives

Your choice of verbs, adverbs and adjectives brings colour and precise detail to your descriptive writing. There is an opportunity here to show the range of your vocabulary, and the following exercises should help you to think about the words you choose when you are describing things. Use a dictionary if you need to find out the meaning of any of the words.

Activity 7

The piece below has had some of the verbs, adverbs and adjectives removed. They are listed in the table below the extract: replace each missing word with the word that you think fits best. You should use all the words to restore the piece of writing to its original form.

A group of girls were VERB around the doorway trying to jump as high as the Easter garland. Their belongings were beside them – a pile of bright, ADJECTIVE lunchboxes and home-made Easter cards with scrawled pink writing, one covered with ADJECTIVE hologram eggs.

5 Outside the gate, one mother was ADVERB trying to gather folders and cigarette packets from the back seat of her car. There were three boys waiting ADVERB next to the Ford Focus. One was pushed off the pavement.

'Boys! Will you behave … now!' hissed the mother ADVERB.

The other two stood ADVERB against the fence. The taller one had orange
10 paint VERB all down the side of one leg.

A line of children followed round the building, uniformed in green 'Class 2' sweatshirts. Some had vibrant yellow, ADJECTIVE chicks while one girl at the back VERB 'Cadbury's' smears from the side of her mouth. The teacher at the front led them to the gate to peer out for their parents. He had a whistle
15 VERB round his neck and was wearing a ADJECTIVE polo shirt with ADJECTIVE trousers. He VERB ADVERB at the assistant by the wall and then returned his attention to the children.

She remained as company for the ADJECTIVE boy. He VERB his feet on the gravel, with one shoelace trailing. The assistant smiled ADVERB then checked
20 her bag for the latest edition of *Cosmopolitan*.

VERBS	ADVERBS	ADJECTIVES
slung	vaguely	shiny
scuffed	hastily	plastic
clustered	cheekily	fluffy
winked	impatiently	loose
dribbled	angrily	small
was licking	meekly	casual

Activity 8

The piece below has also had some of its verbs, adverbs and adjectives removed. Replace the missing words with words from the table that you think fit best. You should use all the words from the table to restore the piece of writing to its original form.

As you ADVERB push open the ADJECTIVE ADJECTIVE doorknob, your nerves are tingling with ADJECTIVE fuelled apprehension, which had begun a moment before as you read the ADVERB painted, ADJECTIVE letters on a ADJECTIVE ADJECTIVE sheet in the window of the little craft shop. You VERB little pinpricks in your skin,
5 but pinpricks so light and feathery, they give a ADJECTIVE ADJECTIVE feeling, and they melt and dissolve as soon as they touch your hands. As you step ADVERB inside onto the ADJECTIVE ADJECTIVE carpet, large clumps of snow are thrown from your well-worn leather boots, and your senses are shattered by the indistinguishable din that confronts you. You are VERB by the creators of this clamour, a vague mass of
10 people, moving everywhere in a frenzy of excitement, rattling around like ants who have chanced upon a feast.

The crowd is VERB among various tables, containing a variety of trinkets to charm their way into your pocket, to be exchanged with the cold, hard metal that jangles so ADVERB in your pocket, clamouring to be spent. Your senses are VERB by a delightful
15 smell of ADJECTIVE coffee, the smell wafting up your nostrils ADVERB. The thick brown liquid VERB down your throat, oozing warmth back to the tips of your fingers which had previously been frozen like icicles, and numb without feeling.

The goods that the shop itself has to VERB are mostly nondescript items, leftovers from the frenzy of Christmas shopping. Among the plastic toys however, there are a
20 few gems. The most prominent of these is a gold brooch, the heavy metal wrought ADVERB into a myriad of complex patterns and shapes, intertwined with pieces of blue glass, the refined cut making the piece VERB as the glass catches the lights on the ceiling, of lapis lazuli, azure and turquoise mirroring ADVERB the gentle waves of the sea. However, this particular delight has not been VERB, unlike the discarded
25 plastic toys. You leave your treasured discovery, its beauty ADVERB hidden among ADJECTIVE junk, and leave, disappointed.

VERBS	ADVERBS	ADJECTIVES
slips	enchantingly	crimson
offer	invitingly	burnished, bronze
aroused	gingerly	excitement-
experience	completely	pleasant, cool
shimmer	warily	frayed, tattered
interspersed	crudely	dirty, torn
reduced	accurately	worthless
greeted	delicately	hot

Descriptive writing key points

The bullet points below are the key points you need to think about to make your descriptive writing successful. You need to follow these and, above all, practise writing descriptively against the clock. You need to experience what 25 minutes feels like when you have got to produce at least a side of writing.

- Write at least one side (no less but not much more).
- Write in sentences, correctly using capital letters and full stops.
- Organise your work into paragraphs (between three and six).
- Pay attention to adverbs and adjectives.
- Think about the verbs you use.
- Try to write from memory rather than imagination.
- Try to include authentic details, including physical description and snatches of dialogue (they don't have to be true, but they do need to be believable).
- Describe, but do not tell a story.
- Avoid the first-person (use the third person, for example).
- Avoid generalisations.
- Focus on the individuals who inhabit the scene.
- Use proper nouns (names of things) where appropriate.

Personal and narrative writing

What will I learn?

In this unit I will:
- learn the techniques used in good narrative writing
- read and discuss examples of narrative writing
- practise a range of narrative writing.

The final question in your English Paper 1 exam, question B2, requires you to write a narrative at least two pages long. A narrative is a continuous account of events. You will be given a list of titles to choose from, and this is the only opportunity you get on either paper to choose what you do. The choice you make needs to be considered carefully, but you have a lot of control over what story you tell and how you tell it.

Approaches to the task

There are three approaches to this task.

1. Your narrative could be **personal**. In other words, it could be based around events that you have taken part in or observed. This is essentially autobiographical writing, but it will almost certainly focus on a particular incident or experience in your life.

   You need to be selective and think about incidents or experiences in your life that might interest or amuse a reader. Imagine if someone asked 'What did you do today?' and you actually told them everything you had done. They would quickly find this very boring! In fact, what they are really asking is 'What did you do today that was of some interest?' You must remember that you have an audience for your writing and it is your job to entertain them.

2. Your narrative could be **imaginative** and **creative**, relying on fiction and your ability to tell a good story. Some people have the ability to create really dramatic and inventive stories, and if you have the flair for this kind of writing, an examiner can reward this. Sometimes it is possible to adapt a basic storyline and make it your own, but it is not a good idea to steal the plot of something you have read or seen on television or in the cinema. Good stories are a delight, but make sure you have a good story to tell.

3. There is also the possibility of mixing **fact** with **fiction** by taking a situation or incident based on real events and adding to it to make it more interesting, exciting or amusing. No one will know, or care, if the apparently 'true' story you are telling has been helped by your imagination. We all have stories to tell and it is good preparation for this part of the exam to think about experiences you have had that might interest someone else.

> ### Remember
>
> You are not writing for yourself. You are writing for your reader and you need to capture their interest. However, you may be surprised by what you can do with an apparently minor incident. Often it is not really the content of a story that makes it succeed, but the way it is told.

The different types of task

There are four different types of title in the exam from which you will have to choose.

1. Continue the story – you are given the opening words to a narrative and asked to continue the tale. You must use the exact words you have been given, and your subsequent narrative must relate to these opening words. For example, do not change third person to first person (or vice versa) so that 'he' or 'she' becomes 'I' within a few lines.

2. Complete the story – in this case you are given the last few words of a narrative and your response must end with these words. Again it is important that you conclude with the exact words you have been given and make sure that the narrative you have written is consistent with this ending. The crucial thing here is planning your narrative so that it reaches exactly the conclusion given. Examiners often say that the last few words seem to be just 'tacked on' and have little to do with what has gone before.

3. Autobiographical – these titles require a personal response which means you are writing about yourself and your feelings, and describing events that you have observed or been involved with. It could be asking you to write about an incident such as 'A time you had to look after a pet', a particular experience such as 'The worst job of my life' or asking you to focus on your feelings such as 'A time you felt justified in breaking the rules'. The best of these are based on real experience and take an honest approach.

4. Open title – this could be a title such as 'The Gamble' or 'The Visitor'. This could lead to an autobiographical response or an imaginative narrative that fits the title.

Tips for succeeding with the personal and narrative writing

- You need to think about openings and endings, particularly when they are given. A good opening can hook the reader and you need to think about how and when to start. Most stories are told in chronological order, but this does not have to be the case. To get the reader thinking and involved, you could start your narrative with a dramatic detail from the end of the narrative or with some vital action from the middle of the story. This can be really effective, but it is important that you structure your response so that the reader is fully aware of what is happening and when it is happening. You need to think about sequencing of events. You should also try to make sure that your narrative reaches a logical conclusion.

- Readers need information, but sometimes a good story withholds information until the appropriate moment. You can create suspense by holding back some information.

- Selecting the material is also important, judging what to put in and what to leave out. Around two sides is the suggested length of this piece of writing, so you must be realistic. You must not attempt too much in the time and space you have available.

- Consistency with characters, names, relationships, tenses and perspective is important. Too many characters make it difficult for the reader to keep track, so it is sensible to avoid stories with a cast of thousands. Your uncle should not become your brother and Charlotte should not turn into Chantelle! It is important to make a conscious decision about using the first or third person. You must then stick with it, unless you are attempting something very ambitious indeed.

- You need to be careful with the 'scale' and 'time-frame' of stories, particularly action stories. A good story is not just a breathless succession of events and, although 'what happens' is part of a good story, we have to care about the characters or be intrigued by the situation. It is not an issue of how much detail you can throw at a topic, but rather how successfully you can *select*. A narrative in which the action takes place 'within an hour' is a good bit of advice. A single incident works well.

- You need to think about the pace of a story, judge when to pause (to comment, reflect or describe) and when to move on.

- Details of people, places and events are necessary to keep the tale interesting, but the narrative must not get bogged down in these details. You need to think about where to put the emphasis in your story.

- Dialogue can be very effective but requires control of layout and punctuation. You can reveal character through dialogue, but if you are not in control of your writing you might make a large number of technical errors. However, avoid using too much dialogue. Do not let your story become a playscript.

Personal writing

In some ways this is the easy option because the material is in your own memory. There are two possible sources for this kind of writing.

1. Experiences of early childhood

This can produce some delightful writing, particularly if you can capture the thoughts and feelings that young children experience. A good memory for detail really helps here.

2. Experiences of your teenage years

This type of writing also allows you to explore your thoughts, feelings and experiences, looking back at fairly recent events but from some distance. This can give a sense of perspective to your writing. Some experiences of three or four years ago may make you cringe with embarrassment, but they could be ideal for a good piece of writing. For example, the Westlife concert you went to when you were twelve may not be something you want to boast about now, but not only could you capture how it felt at the time but also what you feel about the event now. And only the examiner will know!

However, there is no reason why you should not choose to write about some of your recent experiences. They will be fresh in your memory and could provide lots of material for an amusing or interesting piece of writing.

Read the following two pieces of student writing, then complete the activity. The first is an example of early childhood writing; the second is an example of teenage years writing.

Answer 1

I have known Jessi since nursery school. No, before that. Actually we met . . .

Scratch that. I don't remember where we met. Neither do Mum or Dad. It wasn't like they were friends with Jessi's parents or anything. I guess we just met, and decided to be friends.

So.

When we were in the infant class Lila came along. Her mum was friends with my mum, so, of course, Lila and I knew each other. She was American. She was exotic. She was special. Everyone wanted to be her friend.

Except Jessi.

When I visited Lila's house and played with her guinea pigs Louise and Thelma (I begged and begged Mum and Dad to let me have a guinea pig but they said the cats would eat it), Jessi didn't like it.

'You go to her house all the time,' she complained. 'It's not fair.'

I explained, perfectly reasonably I thought, that I had to go to her house because Mum couldn't find me a childminder when she went off to work, and Dad was too busy to have me around. I didn't mention that Lila had the most amazing Barbie set with a horse and carriage and everything, and a collector's edition My Little Pony.

I liked Jessi and I liked Lila. I didn't understand why they couldn't just be friends. Still, even I could see that might be difficult. Lila went swimming and wore baseball caps. Jessi had a bedroom painted pale pink with a pattern of bows along the walls.

I invited both of them to my birthday party in the summer. There were lots of my friends there. We went to the park and played in the playground for hours. As I went on the swings, shrieking to Alex how fun it was, I kept a close eye on them in case there was a scene. There wasn't, but Jessi studiously avoided Lila and Lila only spoke to Jessi once, to ask her to pass the biscuits.

I sighed. I couldn't possibly confront them about it. Maybe the problem would just go away.

It didn't.

Answer 2

A night out. My first in ages. The excitement lit up my face but then worry started to dawn. The image looking back at me wasn't what I wanted to see. 'It's the skirt,' I thought. My dad had always teased me, saying he had to wear sunglasses to look at my legs.

I returned to my wardrobe, now with only a few garments left, the rest strewn across my room. I selected trousers this time. That was better.

On the way in the car, I listened distantly to my mum performing her usual checklist.

'Have you got your phone?'

'Yeh.'

'And you've got credit?'

'Yeh.'

'Remember, eleven at the latest, and if you have any problems, ring.'

'Yeh.'

'Have you eaten?'

'Yeh.'

'Are you even listening to me?'

I'd heard it a thousand times. Take my phone so she can check up on me every five minutes. Eat so it absorbs the alcohol and I won't be so drunk. That was the whole point though, so I never did eat.

Finally, we arrived. There were loads of people, all 'rockers' as we were categorised. I managed to pick out my friends with no problem though. Not many people had a boyfriend with hair waxed up in spikes, inches long. Thank God my mum had learned by now that a goodbye kiss was social suicide for me and I hurried over to the 'gang'. Lauren was wearing a black pleated skirt. It looked lush and a feeling of regret ran through me. I should've worn mine. It was my Dad's fault.

We chatted excitedly as we waited in the queue, knowing that the normal waiting time was approximately an hour.

We waited. A man gave us each a lighter. We waited. Some people pushed in front of us. We waited. Conversation was wearing thin. My makeup began to run as the rain began.

Two hours later, we reached the front. Carys was jumping with excitement. It was her favourite band. My own excited feeling had deteriorated with the wait. I was wet. I wanted to wear my skirt.

This night out seemed destined to fail, as had all my others. I had hyped myself up, only to be let down. I wanted to go home.

Activity 9

Discuss and/or make notes on the following questions about the two stories (on pages 122 and 123), based on the list below.

1. Have the students got stories to tell? What are they?
2. What do you like about the stories?
3. How could they be improved?
4. How effectively do you think the students tell their stories?
5. How are the stories put together?
6. Do the stories start at appropriate places?
7. What do you think of the endings?
8. Are they well written technically?
9. What mistakes in spelling, punctuation or grammar can you find?
10. What do you think is good about the writing? Pick out some examples.

Narrative writing

To help you identify what makes an excellent piece of creative writing, and then to help you improve your own writing, here is an example of an A* piece of creative writing produced in exam conditions. It is creative, ambitious and accurate. Read it through, then complete the activity that follows, which will help to analyse what exactly makes it so good.

He rises at my entrance; how gentlemanly of him, how polite, how greet-the-cash-cow. I smile at him, just barely, showing my teeth. He smiles back genuinely, unflappable.

Creep.

'Hello, Dawn,' he says affably.

5   'Hi,' I reply briefly, taking a look around the office. A chair, a couch, one bookcase-lined wall, one lined with brash certificates preserved carefully in clip frames. I wander over to examine them, pointedly ignoring the genteel, bespectacled man behind me.

Psychology degree from Cambridge. Graduate degree in criminal psychology. British Institute of Psychology. He's a veritable genius of the human mind.

10   Figures.

'Would you like to sit down, Dawn?' he says, and I can tell from his practised calm voice that he's sitting down and waiting to start on me.

'No,' I answer flatly, 'not particularly.'

'Sit down,' he says, in the same I-am-here-to-help tone, but this time there's a hint of
15 steel behind it. I sit, reluctantly, with sighs to show how much I'm put upon.

'I'm Doctor Lee, Dawn,' he tells me. He's obviously been on one of those seminars where they tell you to use someone's name constantly because it forms a connection with them.

'I know,' I say. 'I wanted the other guy.'

'Well, you're here now.'

20 'Yes,' I say precisely, 'under duress. So how about we sit in a nice, calm silence for the hour? You can do some filing or whatever, and you'll still get your money.'

'I'm not in this for the money,' he says, and I'm impressed because he almost looks hurt.

'I'd like to help you, Dawn. Your case is interesting.'

'My case is boring old usual poor little rich girl,' I say. 'Nothing special.'

25 'Yours obviously is special,' he says, reaching for his notes. He consults them, then looks at me seriously over his glasses.

'The poor little rich girl, as you call it, typically wants attention. They attempt to get this in a variety of ways. Criminal activity is one such way. Arson activity,' he looks at me gravely, 'is not the usual form it takes.'

30 'That was never proven,' I say coolly, meeting his gaze.

'It was you and we both know it,' he answers and I'm about to threaten to sue him for slander when he goes on, 'how is Ms Thompson, Dawn?'

I look down, instinctively; when I look back up I hope he didn't catch it but naturally he did. He's smiling. I muster a supercilious smirk back, but I find it hard. I liked Ms Thompson.
35 Like her. She wasn't the point.

'Rec . . .' I say, then have to clear my throat. 'Recovering, I believe.'

'You didn't mean for her to be caught in it,' he states, matter of fact and assured.

I waver; I want to deny it, but to deny that means admitting everything else. I'm damn lucky my father prevented the police investigation from looking to me, because I obviously
40 wouldn't have held up to questioning; one direct question off this man, so unlike my mother sitting on the end of my bed silently crying but never talking to me or my father pretending I'm not there until I just permanently avoid him or my friends looking at me anxiously, suspiciously, smiling falsely to my face and whispering behind my half-turned back – well, I thought that was difficult, but this man wants me to participate in conversation! I'm not sure I remember how.

45 'I don't know what you mean,' I settle for; stalling only, but it'll do. My mind isn't working at its best. He frowns as if he's disappointed (what do I care?) and he reaches for a notepad and pen, flips the cover over and starts writing, slowly and deliberately, on the pad. I wait impatiently.

'You're too smart for complete denial,' he muses, as if I'm not there. 'I thought you'd be
50 too smart for lying.'

I don't answer. I'm not too smart for lying. I'm too used to it for the truth.

'I am here to help you, Dawn,' he asserts, still without looking at me. 'I can help you.'

I wish he'd look up so I can look at his expression; years of my world taught me the body is so much more open than the voice. The voice says it loves you before it leaves on a
55 business trip and doesn't call for a week. The voice says it loves you before it pulls you in and doesn't call at all. The voice cannot be trusted.

Of course, most people, all of them, can't be trusted.

'You're seventeen,' he goes on smoothly. His activity on the pad has stopped, but still he looks down. 'You're not as old as you think you have to be. You can change things now or
60 you can wish you had forever.'

Now he looks up at me and our gazes meet. His is green and warm and intelligent and open, and mine is blurred as the first tear I've cried for years slips softly down my cheek.

Activity 10

We are going to analyse what makes the student's piece of creative writing on pages 124–126 so effective. Perhaps the most interesting feature of the piece is the way it is told. The main 'action' is over before the 'story' begins and the narrative takes place entirely in the doctor's room. The events that led to this confrontation between the narrator and the doctor are gradually revealed, but not everything is clear.

Now answer these questions.
1. What exactly did the narrator burn? Her house? A school? A shop? Another building?
2. Does it affect the story in any way that this information is withheld?
3. Who is Ms Thompson? (She could be a neighbour or a visitor or a cleaner or even a teacher.)
4. Do you think it matters that this is not explained? Do you think it is a strength or a weakness?
5. What has *not* been made clear? Was this careless or was this deliberate?
6. What do you learn about the narrator? How do you learn these things?

7. What do you learn about the doctor? How does the narrator convey this information?

8. What exactly do we find out about the parents of the narrator?

9. How does the writer let us know about the unnamed boyfriend?

10. There are no mistakes in this piece of writing, but there are some unusual features. The writer uses 'single word' sentences at least twice and they are laid out as one-word paragraphs. Why do you think she did it? What do you think of this technique?

11. Which words or phrases do you think are particularly well-chosen? Copy them out. You could add to your vocabulary by looking up in a dictionary the meaning of any unfamiliar words.

Read the following student response on a different task: writing about a visitor. Then complete the activity that follows.

The visitor

It was a dark, misrable night, the rain was coming down like a tone of bricks and lightning as light as the sun on a clear day. I was in my living room watching TV, eating my Pizza which I had just ordered and all of a sudden a large bang came from the front door which was like a firework, it made me jump out of my seat like an olypic hurdler. I slowly and quietly walked to the door like a ninja to see if I could hear and recognise who it was. There was a bang from the door again which shook my windows and made a noise like a rattle snake I finally opened the door very slowly and to my surprise there was a man dressed in a black, he wore black cowboy boots black leather trousers and a leather coat which went all the way down to the floor. He spoke to me in a very deep voice which seemed to echo and said 'My name is Jake my car broke down, please may I use your phone' It took me a long time to awnser him when he came into the light I saw his eyes the were as dark as black whole

Activity 11

The two students' answers (on pages 124–126 and page 127) are quite different in quality. Summarise what you think are the main differences between them. What are the strengths and weaknesses of each piece? You could use the three questions below as headings.

- Does the writer have a story to tell?
- Is the story told well?
- Is it accurate writing?

Examiner tip

You might like to have thought through a 'bank' of ideas or storylines before the exam, to use as starting points when faced with the actual tasks. Think about a few happy, or sad or amusing incidents to work with. This really is time well spent. You don't have to rely on inspiration on the day of the exam!

Activity 12

Now it is your turn to have a go at a piece of narrative writing, entitled: 'The Accident'.

The bullet points below give the bare outline of a plot. You might like to use them as the basis for your piece, or you can use your own ideas.

- Someone is driving home.
- It is night and there is heavy rain.
- There is a high-speed collision with another car.
- The accident is serious and the driver is injured and trapped inside their car, which has left the road.
- A figure appears out of the darkness, but then goes away again.
- The person returns and rescues the trapped driver from the car.
- The injured driver is then driven to hospital by the rescuer.
- Eventually the driver discovers that the journey to the hospital was in a car that was damaged and stolen.

There are several decisions to make here.
- Is this better as a first- or third-person narrative?
- Where would you start?
- How much detail do you need to give about the background and why the narrator is driving home at night?
- How much detail do you provide about the actual collision?
- How much space do you give to the time in the car when the driver is trapped and injured?
- Why does the other character go away and then return? Have you guessed who it is? How do you suggest who he is without actually saying so?
- How do you handle the way the narrator discovers that the 'rescuer' was in a stolen and damaged car?

What have I learnt?

In this section we covered:
- techniques used in good descriptive writing, including:
    writing in sentences
    using verbs, adverbs and adjectives
- techniques used in good personal and narrative writing, including:
    imaginative and creative approaches
    writing from personal experience
    types of Paper 1 Section B exam questions.

How confident do you now feel about each of the above? You could note down the points you feel confident about and those you need to go back to.

Introduction

What will Section B of Paper 2 look like?

In Section B of Paper 2 you have about 70 minutes to tackle two pieces of transactional writing – writing that pays special attention to audience, purpose and format. Both answers will be marked out of 20. You will be asked to write two of the following: a letter, a report, an article, a leaflet, a speech or a review.

In this section you will also be assessed for your writing skills, including the presentation of your work, spelling, punctuation and layout.

What will the questions be like?

The questions will test your ability to:
- argue, persuade, advise
- analyse, review, comment.

One question will test your ability to argue, persuade, or advise; and the other your ability to analyse, review, or comment. One will be linked to the Reading passages in Section A, so for example if the passages are based on circuses you might be asked to write a letter to a newspaper, giving your opinion on whether they should be allowed to continue.

What should I do?

- Read the instructions carefully – they are there to help you.
- Divide your time equally – about 35 minutes per question – and make sure that your answers are about the length suggested.
- Read the questions carefully and make sure that you answer the question set.
- Think carefully before you write – plan what you will say in your introduction, in each paragraph and in the conclusion.
- When you have finished writing, read through and check for errors – don't be afraid to make changes if they will improve your work.

Paper 2 Section B sample questions

Informal letters

You have a friend who has decided to run in the London Marathon. Write a letter to your friend, giving your opinions.

Formal letters

Because of falling numbers the council is considering closing your school and joining it with a school 5 miles away. Write a letter to the local newspaper, giving your views.

Reports

1. Your school council has asked you to write a report on the IT facilities in your school. This report is to be presented to the head teacher.
2. Following a meeting the young people of your community have been asked to write a report and recommendations for the local council on facilities/activities available for teenagers in the area. Write the report.

Articles for newspapers and magazines

1. Write an article for a travel magazine about a place that you think would be good to visit for a holiday, either in the UK or abroad.
2. Write an article for your school magazine entitled 'Sporting opportunities in this school'.

Leaflets

1. Write a leaflet designed to attract teenagers to a theme park.
2. Write a leaflet telling Year 7 pupils what they need to know about their new school.

Speeches

1. As part of your speaking and listening activities it is your turn to address your class. The topic you have chosen is 'Should mobile phones be allowed in school?'
2. A local business sponsored you to visit a town of your choice. On your return you have been asked to tell them about your trip. Write what you would say.

Reviews

1. Write an entry for a guide book about a place you know well, including details about obvious as well as less obvious sights. You can be both positive and negative.
2. Write a review of a recent television programme you enjoyed. Your review is intended for a newspaper and can, of course, include less successful aspects of the programme.

Transactional writing

Audience, purpose and format

In transactional writing there is an emphasis on audience and purpose and, in some cases, layout. So what do we mean by these three things?

Audience

Audience means who this piece of writing is intended for – a friend, an employer, a newspaper/magazine reader, a potential customer, etc. What you write and the way you write it will depend on who the reader is. For a friend, your tone will be friendly, chatty and informal (though bearing in mind that you are writing in an exam). For an employer, on the other hand, you will adopt a more serious or formal tone.

Purpose

Purpose means the reason behind the piece of writing – for example, to argue, persuade, comment or review. You may write a letter to make contact with a friend you have not seen for some time, or write an article for a teenage magazine to give your views on films, fashion, music, etc. You may be required to write a leaflet or fact sheet telling people about an issue that interests you.

Format

'Format' means how you set something out. When writing a letter you should take care to put the address(es) in the right place, include the date, provide a greeting (a salutation such as 'Dear') and an ending or closure. A report contains headings and sub-headings so that different topics are dealt with separately and the report is easier for the reader to follow. Similarly, newspaper/magazine articles, leaflets, factsheets and reviews would have headings (possibly catchy ones) and perhaps sub-sections. Photographs/diagrams may be used (you don't need to draw them but you might like to indicate where you would place them).

Informal letters

An informal letter is probably one written to a friend or a member of your family. Because you know the person well you will use a friendly approach and the letter may have a chatty tone.

Below is an example of the layout of an informal letter. The annotations show some of the common features you will need to use.

Your address.

> 10 Grange Road
> Leeds
> LS6 4PT

The date.

> 16th April 2007

Greeting (salutation).

> Dear Sam,

Short introductory paragraph.

Purpose of the letter.

> I can't believe that you're planning on uprooting and going to live in Spain. I can understand your Dad wanting to get away from being an accountant in Slough but what about the effects on you?

Three or four middle paragraphs that cover the points you wish to make.

> --
> --

The letter will end with a brief but important closing paragraph that will round off the purpose of the letter.

> I hope I haven't been too cruel in what I've said. I'm just concerned as your friend that this is the wrong move for you and your family. 'There's no going back' as they say. I hope your Dad thinks carefully about this.
> Love,
> Amanda

Informal closure.   Your first name.

Look at a letter written by a student in an exam. The task the students had to complete was:

You have a friend or relative who is considering moving abroad. **Write a letter giving your opinions.**

14th June 2007

Dear Sarah

After recently listening to you talk about going to live abroad I have been thinking about how my life will change without you.

We first met in high school where we were very close friends then we went to college we lost touch, and now I feel I have just got my best friend back and you are talking about moving abroad.

At times I envy you because you have got a big caring family, a nice house, a very good job and a caring partner. Why do you want to leave all this behind to live abroad?

I have got so many great memories, especially your sister's wedding where we danced till 2 the following day and that weird barman came on to me, that was just embarrassing!

Going abroad to live is a very big step you will have to find a job and accomodation and a set of new friends. As you know I disagree very much with you moving away but at the end of the day it is your decision and future.

I hope whichever decision you make is the right one and will make you happy!
Good Luck!

Yours faithfully

Jackie

Activity 1

Now you are going to evaluate the letter on page 134. To do this you should think about the following.

- Layout (address, date, salutation, closure) – are they appropriate/in the right places?
- Organisation – introduction, paragraphing and the conclusion.
- Content – does the letter say the sort of things you would expect?
- Tone – does it sound like a letter to a friend? Pick out examples where it is successful and less successful.
- Technical errors (such as spelling mistakes) and successes.

Activity 2

The fifth paragraph in the letter on page 134, beginning 'Going abroad to live …', deals briefly with some of the problems the writer feels her friend will encounter.

Re-write this paragraph, giving details about the difficulties of finding a job and accommodation, and making new friends.

Activity 3

Complete your own informal letter.

Your uncle and aunt have won some money on the National Lottery. They wish to share their good fortune with you and have sent you a cheque for £500.

Plan your letter of thanks to them. It should include details of how you intend to spend the money. Remember also to include:

- your address, the date, the salutation and a closure
- an opening paragraph
- three or four middle paragraphs
- a closing paragraph.

Remember

Always make your letter suitable for the person receiving it. A letter to a close friend will not sound the same or have the same sort of content as a letter to, for example, your grandma.

Examiner tip

When tackling a piece of writing of this sort, always bear in mind these things.

- Purpose: Why am I writing this piece?
- Audience: Who is it written for?
- Format: How should my work be set out?

Formal letters

Audience

A formal letter is one that you write to a person you may not know personally or who you may know in a more formal way. It could be a potential employer, a doctor, a newspaper editor, or a head teacher. This will obviously influence the way in which your letter is written. The language and tone will be formal and quite different from the conversational style of the informal letters we have looked at so far. Most letters of this type take a fairly serious approach.

Purpose

The purpose of the letter may be to raise and comment on an issue, to make suggestions, to apply for a job, etc. Whatever the purpose, it is important that an appropriate tone is used. If writing on an issue that is of concern to you, you may, of course, express those views strongly and forcefully, but you should always remain polite.

Format

Another big difference between formal and informal letters is the format. Again, you will include your address and the date, but this time you will also include the address of the person you are writing to and the salutation will be more formal, e.g. 'Dear Mrs Fletcher', or 'Dear Sir/Madam' if you do not know the name of the person. In the exam you may be given the address; if not, you can make one up. The closure if you do not know the person's name will be 'Yours faithfully'. If you started the letter with a name, e.g. 'Dear Mrs Sullivan', then you would end the letter 'Yours sincerely'.

Content

The content of the letter will be determined by the topic you are asked to write on. But whatever the topic is, you must plan your answer. Think of the central points you wish to make and how you intend to argue them. Arguing or putting your points across logically is important, and justifying what you say strengthens your case. The organisation will be very similar to that suggested for the informal letter:

- a fairly brief opening paragraph outlining your reason for writing
- three or four central paragraphs in which you put your case
- a final paragraph that rounds off the letter.

Activity 4

You have been asked to write a letter to your local council, persuading it to support a project in your area. Think of a suitable project, then plan your answer either on your own or with a partner. First, indicate how you would set out the letter. Then:

- write your opening paragraph
- outline the arguments you will put forward in your central paragraphs, but don't write the detail
- write a closing paragraph that will round off your letter.

On page 138 there is an example of a formal letter written by a student under exam conditions. Read the letter, then complete the activity that follows. The task the student had to complete was:

A local hotel/restaurant owner is advertising for part-time staff. Write a letter applying for the job.

The Bridge Hotel

16 Wharley Road

Birmingham

Jane Tingle

65 Hinton Rd

Birmingham

BR3 8PL

Tel: 07882 462941

11th March 2007

Dear Mrs Jennings

I am writing to apply for the part time job at your hotel. I saw the advertisement in the local paper and thought that I would be well suited for the job.

I am 18 years of age and have just moved to this area to follow a catering course at the local college. I am a reliable and consientious worker with good personal skills. I get on well with people and have experienced no problems in working relationships in the past.

I have worked in a hotel before and was complemented for my commitment and hard work. I have experience of the full range of hotel work and enjoyed all the tasks given to me. What I especially enjoyed was the chance to meet so many different people and to help them with their requests.

While at my previous job I went on a customer relations course which enabled me to learn how to take care of situations which may arise in my day to day work. This would be helpful to me if I was to get this job.

I am available for interview at any time convenient to you and I would be happy to answer any questions you may have. I can be contacted at the address or phone number at the top of this letter.

I look forward to hearing from you.

Yours faithfully,

Jane Tingle

Activity 5

In pairs, discuss the letter on page 138. How successful has the student been in completing the task (see page 137)? To frame your discussion you could focus on the following.

- The layout and organisation – what works well and what does not?
- The tone – if you were the hotel owner would you think it polite and respectful?
- The case she puts for herself – is the supporting information relevant to this job?
- How accurately it is written.

What grade do you think this letter would get?

Activity 6

Using what you have learnt in this section, write a formal letter. Either complete the letter to the council that you started to plan for Activity 4, or write a formal letter in response to the task below:

A local hotel/restaurant owner is advertising for part-time staff. Write a letter applying for the job.

Remember to:
- set out your letter correctly
- plan what will be included in each paragraph
- take care with spelling, punctuation and grammar.

Reports

Purpose

The purpose of a report is to inform, advise or persuade a person or a group of people. It is normally written after something has been investigated/thought about – for example, the state of a school's facilities or leisure opportunities for young people in a community. It gives up-to-date information to those who need the information and can act on it.

Format

There will be a clear and straightforward format so that the points raised are presented clearly to the reader(s). There will be a main heading and probably sub-headings, since the report is likely to consider different aspects of the subject. The clear separation of these aspects will help the reader(s) and will give shape and organisation to your work.

Audience

In general, reports tend to be formal. In the exam you will be told who the report is for, such as members of your school council or maybe your local council. The stated audience will, of course, help you to decide how the report is to be written. It will be more formal for the local council than for your fellow students, but even in this case there will be some formality.

Tone

The tone will be polite, but do not be afraid to put your views in a strong way. Making your points forcefully is not the same as being rude. Your points should be based on evidence and need to be clearly put across.

Planning and writing your report

The following stages should help you to plan and write your report.

1. Make sure you understand exactly what you are being asked to do. Ask yourself these questions.
   - What is the report about?
   - Who is it for?
2. Write a heading. It can be straightforward or, if a suitable idea occurs to you, catchy.
3. Under the heading 'Introduction', briefly explain the background and purpose of your report.
4. Think about what areas you want to cover and choose sub-headings for them.
5. Under the heading 'Conclusion', briefly draw together your findings and make recommendations. You must be sensible and realistic if you want your report to be carefully considered. Your conclusion can be effective at persuading your reader.

> **Examiner tip**
>
> Rather than writing 'The first (or second, etc.) point I will make is …', try to use words such as 'Importantly' or 'Crucially' or 'Equally'. This will make your writing more interesting and gain a higher mark.

> **Examiner tip**
>
> Presenting your recommendations as a list of bullet points can be effective.

> **Activity 7**
>
> You have been asked by the school council to write a report suggesting how your school's facilities could be improved.
> 1. Write your introduction.
> 2. Write a list of sub-headings that you would include in your report – but don't write the detail yet.
> 3. Write the concluding paragraph.

On page 141 is a student's response to the task:
Write a report on the effectiveness of transport facilities in your area.

Read the report, then complete Activity 8.

HOW EFFECTIVE ARE TRANSPORT FACILITIES IN THE NANTWICH AREA?

<u>Introduction:</u> Nantwich is a town of around 20,000 people situated in South Cheshire. This report will describe the different types of transport in the area.

BUS SERVICES

Local Bus Services

The area is served mainly by the local bus company Crosville. There are regular services to local towns such as Crewe, Chester and Middlewich. Buses to the local villages run less frequently – once a day in some areas but only once a week to some of the smaller rural communities. Most people are generally happy with the bus service but some complained that bus services to the outlying rural areas were too infrequent.

National Bus Service

A National Express coach which travels between Liverpool and London stops at Nantwich twice a week.

RAILWAY SERVICES

Nantwich has a railway station which is on the mainline route from Manchester to Cardiff. Trains regularly pass through the station but only stop four times a day in either direction. Crewe Station is 5 miles from Nantwich and is a mainline station. Some people complain that the train service to Crewe is not frequent enough and is unreliable.

AIR TRAVEL

Nantwich is 35 miles from Manchester Airport which is a major International airport. Trains run regularly from Crewe to Manchester Airport. A road journey to the airport takes approximately 45 minutes.

ROADS AND MOTORWAYS

Nantwich is 8 miles from the M6 motorway. There are good road links with nearby towns and traffic congestion only occurs at rush hour. There have been a number of complaints that minor roads in the area are in a poor state of repair.

CYCLE WAYS

There are no cycle paths in the local area. This is unfortunate because the area around the town is flat and good for cycling.

CONCLUSIONS

For a town of its size Nantwich has good transport links. It is situated close to a big railway station, airport and a major motorway. Local transport is less good and transport links with villages in the area need to be improved.

Activity 8

In pairs, use the questions below to decide how good the report on page 141 is – you could try to give it a grade.

1. Did the student understand exactly what they were being asked to do? To answer this, think about whether it is clear what the report is about and who it has been written for.
2. Is the heading effective and/or catchy? Why?
3. How clear is the Introduction about the report's background and purpose?
4. How effectively does the student cover the main points they make? Are the sub-headings effective?
5. How effectively does the Conclusion draw the findings together? Does it make recommendations?
6. Overall, how effective do you think the report is, and why?

Activity 9

Now it is your chance to write a report of your own in full. You could *either* complete the school council report you planned in Activity 4, *or* write a report on the following.

There is a lot of debate about the use of mobile phones in schools. Write a report for your headteacher about how they should be handled in your school.

Think about:
*   what is happening at present
*   changes that should be made.

Remember to:
*   start with an introduction
*   use suitable sub-headings
*   write a conclusion and your recommendations.

Examiner tip

A report that is helpfully set out will be more effective and will get you a better mark in the exam.

Articles for magazines and newspapers

Articles tend to be written for newspapers and magazines. If you are asked to write one, you should be clear about its purpose, audience and format.

Purpose

In most cases a magazine or newspaper article is written to inform, persuade and entertain. To achieve these aims, most articles need to be written in a lively style and contain interesting facts and probably opinions. You may hold any opinion you like, but your case must be argued convincingly and clearly.

Audience

The style and tone of an article written for a school magazine will be different from that for a national or local newspaper. An exam question asking you to write an article will tell you the type of publication the article is for and the intended audience.

Format

This is quite straightforward. An article usually needs a main heading that makes it clear what the article is about. The use of paragraphs is important. They will give structure to your article.

What makes a good article?

An effective article is carefully written, interests its readers, informs them, makes them think and causes them to react. This can be achieved in a number of ways.

- Choose a subject that is interesting and topical. Subjects being talked about at the present time are likely to be of more interest than those that have become dated.
- Choose your topic carefully and be selective. If, for example, you are writing an article for a travel magazine on London, you cannot possibly cover everything. So think carefully before writing about the things you would want to include.
- Use a style and devices that make the article lively. This will depend on the publication and audience. You may wish to be informal and chatty, to use questions to draw the reader in, to repeat a word or phrase for effect, to use irony or sarcasm, to make bold statements in order to shock, etc.
- Organise your material in a purposeful way with:
  a catchy heading
  an introduction that immediately draws the reader's attention, perhaps using a question
  three or four central paragraphs
  a short but effective conclusion.

> **Remember**
>
> Your use of language, sentence structure and technical accuracy affect the mark you will get.

Activity 10

You have been asked to write an article entitled 'Eating in Britain today' for a teenage magazine. Write just the outline plan for your article. It should include:
- a title
- an opening paragraph
- an indication of what your three or four middle paragraphs would contain
- a conclusion.

Newspapers and magazines often have articles about places to visit. The article on page 145 was written in response to the question:

A travel magazine has asked for articles about places that offer a good holiday in Britain or abroad. Write an article based on a place of your choice.

Answer 1

Barcalona

The city of Barcelona offers you a great family holiday. There is the home of the Barcelona football team the [Neu Camp] which is europes largest stadium. Also right next door is the wonderful muesium which consists of the Barcelona trophy cabinet which includes the 1992 european trophy.

Barcelona also have the olympic stadium which hosts Barcelona's bitter rivals Espanyol and was the venue for the 1992 olympic Games.

There is (a) also wonderful shopping options, take a trip down the world famous la Rambla and the human statues first hand. Not too far from there is wonderful Barcelona Zoo which has Europes only Albeano Gorilla, Snowflake.

Also in the centre of Barcelona is the building that has taken hundred and fifty years to build and is still not finished.

If that is not enough for you there is the nighttime Barcelona fountains which has beautiful laser coloured lights along with wonderful fountains. All this has simple and easy access with their fantastic underground metro system which was made for the 1992 olympic games, where the villiage is still there for all to see.

If it is just the quiet, relaxing holiday then you are neaver far from a beach along the costa delsol. Which can boast loverly blue sea to go along with the shingle beaches available.

Go on treat yourself.

Activity 11

The article on page 145 was awarded a Grade D in the exam.

1. Using the headings below as a starting point, discuss its good and bad points and how the student might have achieved a better grade.
   - Introduction
   - Paragraphing
   - Conclusion
   - Content
   - Spelling, grammar and punctuation
2. Choose one of the paragraphs from the article and re-write it. Improve it, using the points you have just discussed.

Answer 2 on page 147, also written by a student, is similar in type to the piece on Barcelona. It is slightly different, because this task asked for an article about a tourist attraction. Read the answer, then complete the activity that follows. Note: this is only part of the student's answer.

Answer 2

The Connaught Gardens

The seaside town of Sidmouth nestles between two great cliffs in picturesque Lyme Bay. It takes just five minutes' walk from the town's main bus station, along the Victorian-built Esplanade, to reach the Connaught Gardens from where there is a delightful view over the whole of the beautiful Regency town.

Named after the Duke of Connaught, the Connaught Gardens have associations with many royal figures, most notably Queen Victoria who frequently visited Sidmouth in her childhood. The Victoria Rose Garden, the pride of the Connaught Gardens, is dedicated to her memory and boasts an all-weather visitors' centre with exhibitions of photographs and clothes from the time, as well as an exquisite and astounding display of hundreds of different varieties of rose. After you've looked at the original Victorian maps and manuscripts, a walk through the shady and scented orchard will take you to what locals call 'Paradise House', where exotic plants from all over the world will delight you as you walk along the sand. In winter there are free cider and apple juice tastings here, with the opportunity to take home a bottle all year round from the visitors' centre.

There really is something to delight everyone in the Connaught Gardens. Children are encouraged to take part in the free activities held during Sidmouth's annual folk festival, including dance, drama and art and crafts. Everywhere is suitable for wheelchair users and there is a full range of disabled facilities, including special seating for disabled people and their families in the Clock Tower Tea Rooms. Set in a real working clock tower with a brass bell these tea rooms are cosy and welcoming, with plenty of menu choice. Why not try the delicious and traditional Devon Cream Tea, or perhaps a hearty slice of homemade cake?

Take a step back in time, effortlessly and in tranquil surroundings. We hope to see you soon!

Activity 12

The answer on page 147 is a much better piece of writing than the one on Barcelona (on page 145). In pairs, write down the reasons why this is so. You could suggest what grade it is worth. Use the following headings.

- Content
- Organisation
- Writing skills
- Technical accuracy

Activity 13

Now it's your turn to write an article. You could *either* complete your piece on eating in Britain today (Activity 10, page 144), *or* complete the following:

Write a magazine article, aimed at families, on activities or entertainment in your area. You could be complimentary or critical or a mixture of both.

Remember

An article for a newspaper or magazine should be informative, interesting and accurately written.

Leaflets

When you walk into motorway services, hotels and doctors' surgeries you often see a display of leaflets. When you look at examples of leaflets, look carefully at their features. You will notice:

- they are usually glossy
- they are usually colourful
- they are neatly presented
- they contain a mixture of text, photos, diagrams.

Obviously in an exam you cannot produce a leaflet in this way, but you can show that you:

- understand their purpose
- can write for an appropriate audience
- can adopt the right tone and style
- can use some of the format features.

Purpose

So what is the purpose of a leaflet? It is to inform, advise and persuade. It could be written to encourage people to consider certain issues such as health, and to encourage them to change their behaviour – for example, to stop smoking or eat less junk food. One of the most common uses of a leaflet is to advertise interesting places to visit, such as a theme park or a castle.

Audience

The audience will vary: a leaflet on quad bike facilities might be aimed at younger people, while a visit to a stately home might be targeted more at adults. But remember that in many cases leaflets will attempt to attract as wide an audience as possible.

Tone and style

The tone and style of a leaflet can be formal or informal, or a mixture of both. It should be lively and interesting.

Format

The format of a leaflet is important, but this will vary. However, it should present information in a way that makes it easy to find in the leaflet and must capture the interest of the reader. If you collect some leaflets, look at what format features they contain.

Features of a well–designed leaflet

The following list should help you to remember the main features of a leaflet that has been designed effectively. They usually include the following.
1. A heading that makes it clear what the leaflet is about.
2. Sub-headings or sections so that information can be easily located.
3. Bullet points – these help to make it more attractive and give variety.
4. Pictures – remember, though, that in the exam you are given credit for what you write, not for your ability as an artist. You can, however, indicate where drawings might appear in your leaflet.

Read the extract on page 151, then complete Activity 14 on page 152. The extract is from an NHS leaflet about the dangers of being exposed to too much sun.

Sun Facts – the BURNING issues

The sun makes us feel happy and relaxed, improves our mood and provides essential vitamins to help keep our bodies healthy. However, over-exposure to harmful sunrays, especially when we are young, can damage the skin and lead to skin cancer.

- **Sunscreen**
  Use a sunscreen SPF 15 or higher, with UVA protection, apply generously and often, especially to exposed skin. Always reapply after swimming. Remember, protection is not just for holidays. You can burn even in the UK on a cloudy day. Relying on sun creams to prolong time spent in the sun can increase your overall exposure to the sun and the risk of skin cancer.

- **Cover up**
  Wear loose-fitting clothing made from tightly woven natural fibres to protect skin from the sun's rays. Wear a wide-brimmed hat to shade the face and for the eyes wear sunglasses that are British/European standard approved. Resist the temptation to 'strip off' when it is hot and sunny; always stay covered up. If your hair is thinning or closely 'cropped' in style, be sure to protect your scalp, ears and neck.

- **Drink water**
  Aim to drink at least 6–8 glasses or more of water a day, especially in hot weather. Water helps you to stay fit and refreshed, have healthier skin and fresher breath, and have better concentration. Dehydration can cause headaches, fatigue, depression, dry skin, constipation and kidney problems. Water from the tap is inexpensive and good for you. Try chilling a bottle of tap water in the fridge, it tastes good and is always ready for use. When holidaying abroad drink bottled water. Drink more; don't wait until you are thirsty!

- **Sun beds**
  Avoid using sun beds as these are not safer than being exposed to the sun's rays. A sun bed tan gives little or no protection against sunburn and causes premature ageing of the skin. Excessive use of sun beds or lamps may lead to skin cancer.

Too much sun can cause skin cancer, premature ageing, wrinkles, heat exhaustion and sunstroke.

Activity 14

Look carefully at the NHS leaflet on page 151 and answer the following questions.
1. What is the purpose of this leaflet?
2. Who is it intended for (its audience)?
3. How well does it match the features of a well-designed leaflet? Does it include the following?
   - A heading that makes it clear what the leaflet is about.
   - Sub-headings or sections so that information can be easily located.
   - Bullet points to help to make it more attractive and give variety.
   - Effective pictures.

The example below was produced by a student. Read it, then read what the examiner thought (page 153). The task the student had to complete was:

Your school or college is running a campaign during Healthy Eating Week to persuade students to buy and eat more fruit. It has asked you to produce a leaflet that will be given out in the dining hall.

Healthy Eating Week is Here Pupils!

Here it is – school healthy eating week has finally arrived. We would wish to ask you to support your school and bodies! This week in engaging in eating healthily with fruit!

In our school I have seen a plague of high fattening food. Pupil becoming infected with the amount of fats in food. It is time to put a stop to this, and fruit is the cure.

Fruit such as bananas, oranges, apples are all healthy. They are very tasty and can satisfy your hunger needs while also being scrumptious.

Food is available in the cafeteria, and the New Healthy eating tuck shop. But also why not bring food from home as long as it is healthy food such as fruit we don't care!

Fruit such as bananas are vital to maintain fitness, so all you sports liking kids start getting some.

Fruit and other healthy eating foods give a good supply of energy, fibre and vitamins. All the ingredients for a healthy body. Healthy foods eaten this week should be low in calories.

SICK of Eating High Cholesteral food then why not join in?

We have the resources and the food so why not give in and become a healthier person.

Healthy sportsmen such as Tiger Woods eat healthy fruit as it will improve your stamina and game greatly.

Why not join in its simple and healthy. I would rather be healthy than not woulde'nt you?

What did the examiner think?

Let's look at the good points first.
- The student sticks to the topic.
- The style and tone are suitable for the stated audience: 'to support your school', 'satisfy your hunger needs'.
- The writer does try to persuade the audience, e.g. use of emotive words like 'plague', 'infected', 'tasty', etc.
- It sounds sensible: 'why not bring food from home'.
- Uses examples, e.g. Tiger Woods.
- Uses questions.
- An attempt has been made to set it out as a leaflet.
- It has shape, i.e. an introduction, the main points and a strong finish with a rhetorical question.

How could it be improved? By taking more care with:
- spelling
- sentences
- planning and organisation.

Remember

A rhetorical question is a question where the answer is obvious so does not need to be said. It can be an effective persuasive technique.

Activity 15

See if you can find places where the spelling, sentences and planning/organisation need improving in the 'Healthy eating week' leaflet on page 152. For each example, either put in the correct answer or suggest what you would do that would improve the original version. You could use a table like the one below to record your points.

Point to be improved on	Correction or suggested improvement	How does the change improve the piece?
Spelling/punctuation	Greatly (not greatly)	It is now accurate.
Sentences		
Organisation	Fruit could be dealt with in one paragraph/section.	

Activity 16

Write a leaflet for eleven to twelve-year-olds, encouraging them not to start smoking. Before starting to write, think carefully about what you want to say and how you can set your leaflet out effectively.

- Think of a catchy or shocking title.
- Address your audience.
- Ask them questions, such as 'Did you know that …'.
- Include some statistics or evidence.
- Appeal to their good sense.
- Use a mixture of reason and (possibly) shock tactics.
- Use rhetorical questions such as 'Is it ever too late to give up?'.
- Use a mix of presentation skills, e.g. varying sentence and paragraph length, using bullets.
- Try to end with a telling, punchy conclusion that will stay in the reader's mind.

Examiner tip

Your leaflet should be about one to one-and-a-half sides in length. You may use columns if you wish.

Writing a speech

An exam question that asks you to write a speech will tell you the purpose of the speech and the audience to write for.

Purpose

The purpose of a speech is to give information, to raise issues and to advise and/or persuade. The precise emphasis may be different, depending on circumstances. A politician's emphasis will be on persuasion, whereas a scientist might concentrate on giving information and raising issues.

Audience

In the exam the audience will be made clear to you; this is a vital piece of information. If you write a speech for a group of young children, its content and style will be different from a speech for your peers and different again from one given to members of the Rotary Club or retired businesspeople.

Tone

While it will be polite, the tone will vary depending on the audience you are asked to address. If you are talking to your class, it may be less formal and more chatty than if you are addressing adults. If it is a contribution to a phone-in, it will probably be less formal.

Planning and writing a speech

The following steps will help you to plan and write a speech.
1. Open with a welcome/greeting to your audience. This will be brief and simple – 'Good afternoon ladies and gentlemen' or 'Fellow classmates …'.
2. Outline what the speech will be about: 'I intend to demonstrate that raising the driving age to 18 is unjust' or 'My intention is to try to persuade you that it is right to ban smoking in all public places'.
3. Make three or four key points and expand on them. The choice of material is up to you, but remember that you are trying to keep the attention of your audience and you may be attempting to win them over to your point of view. Try to provide evidence for what you say.
4. Write a conclusion that will hopefully have an impact on the audience.
5. End with an acknowledgement of the audience, such as: 'Thank you for listening.'

In preparing your speech, you should think of ways of winning your audience over. Some of these might be:

- adopting the right tone
- using rhetorical devices such as 'I am sure you will agree that ...', 'Some people might say that ...', 'It is often claimed ...', 'Would you be prepared to, ...'
- using humour
- using repetition (though not overdoing it) 'My opponents say that ... they say ... they say ...'
- using statistics (but not too many)
- coming up with a memorable phrase or two
- using personal experience
- being deliberately controversial.

> ### Remember
>
> You can inform and persuade in many different ways. The list opposite will help you.

Activity 17

A local radio station has asked for extended contributions from listeners on the subject of lowering the legal age for drinking to sixteen or raising it to 21. Your task is to plan the speech you would give on the radio programme. In your plan you should do the following.

- Write your introduction. This should be about three or four lines in length and should outline the case you wish to make, e.g. 'I am sixteen years of age and am fed up with being treated like a child. Surely it is time that we looked again at the legal age for drinking alcohol. The present arrangements are unfair and unsuitable for people of my age living in 2007.'
- List the three or four central points you will make. In writing your speech you should give one paragraph to each main point you make.
- Write your conclusion. Like the introduction, this will be quite brief, i.e. about three or four lines. Do not repeat what you have said, but sum up and round off your speech, e.g. 'These are the main reasons I feel as I do and I am sure that many people (or some of you) support my views. Isn't it now time to change the old-fashioned rules so that they reflect the times we live in?'

Then, with a partner, discuss the main points you would make – in particular how to develop the second bullet point.

Below is an example of a student's speech. The task was to write a contribution to a radio phone-in on the use of animals in circuses.

The student has made their views clear and the answer does have strengths. Read the speech, then complete Activity 18 that follows.

Hello my name is Ben Smith and I am phoning in to say how disgusted I am with Animal circuses.

I do not know how people can go and watch these shows which scream out animal cruelty.

These circus owners are using animals which cannot talk or make their own decisions. Animals are locked up like criminals on a life sentence just so that he/she can make some money.

Do these people have any heart? If the roles were changed I am sure they would feel lonely, chained, disoriented and feel a lot of injustice.

I believe that no animal deserves to be chained up and made to do silly tricks for the amusement of human beings.

We as human beings should feel disgusted in ourselves as we have been given the role of domination over the animals and are now abusing it.

Yes I have had pets who have lived in cages such as my two guinie pigs but at least they got to run around the garden each day and have some exercise. Here we are talking about big animals/wild animals who are used to their natral habitat. These animals are not for taming they are here to live their own lives and we are abusing that.

By people going to these circuses they are incouraging these circus owners to keep on going and to keep on making money out of these animals.

We have to stop it now. I respect organisations like the R.S.P.C.A. for their work and commitment and I am sure if we all lend a hand we can abolish this sick business.

Activity 18

1. Use the following headings to assesss the speech you have just read (on page 157).
   - Good features
   - Things that could be improved
   - The opening/welcome/greeting
   - The outline of what the speech is about
   - The main points made
   - The conclusion
   - Paragraphing
   - Accuracy

2. What grade would you have awarded for this in the exam? Think about:
   - the ideas
   - the organisation of the ideas
   - the technical accuracy.

Activity 19

You have been asked by your English teacher to give a class talk. You have a free choice of subjects. You could *either* choose to complete the 'drinking age' speech you started to plan in Activity 17 (page 156) *or* choose a new topic. Write out your speech. Remember to:

- choose a subject you are familiar with
- keep your audience in mind throughout
- keep the interest of the listeners
- organise your thoughts carefully
- link the points you make
- use devices such as repetition, questions, etc where appropriate.

Don't forget that planning and organisation are important and you must interest your audience.

Reviews

Many of us enjoy watching films, then talking about them with friends and giving opinions. When you do this you are reviewing in an informal way. It is not a big jump from that to creating a written review.

Purpose

The purpose of a review is to give a critical opinion of a book, film, piece of music or CD, television programme, play, etc. Reviews might appear in a magazine or newspaper. They vary in length, but you should be able to complete the task on one side of a page of your exam answer book. Remember, a review is not retelling a story: you don't want to spoil other people's enjoyment.

Format

The main format feature in many reviews is a heading. A review will have a clear structure: an introduction to the book, film or CD, followed by paragraphs that discuss it. Finally, there will be an overall opinion and recommendation. A star rating (i.e. one to five stars) may also be included. Details such as a book's publisher or the name of the music company need to be included.

Audience

This section on transactional writing has stressed the importance of audience. Audience is also important in a review: what you write and the way you write it will vary, depending on who you are writing for. The style of a review written for a teenage magazine will be different from one written for *The Times* newspaper, for example.

Main features of a review

Most reviews have the following features in common.
- A heading, often the name of a book, film or CD.
- An introduction that will tell the reader something general, such as: 'This is the latest book in the series by this author and continues the fascinating adventures of the central character …'
- Middle paragraphs that discuss the CD, book or film in more detail, indicating what the listener, reader or filmgoer can expect (without giving too much away in the case of a novel or film).
- An opinion and perhaps comparison with other work by the same artist(s). There could also be a recommendation and, perhaps, a star rating.

> **Examiner tip**
>
> If a review is set in the exam you can choose the CD, film, book or TV programme you would like to write about. Don't choose what you think the examiner will approve of; choose something you know well and that interests you. The best reviews come from students who clearly know their chosen subject.

Music reviews

Music reviews give opinions on all forms of music. They are likely to deal with an album as a whole, as well as giving opinions on individual tracks. They may refer to other songs or albums by the same artist.

Below is a review of an Oasis album, written by a student under exam conditions. It is intended for a teenage audience. Discuss what you think of the review, then read what the examiner thought.

> Anyone wondered what the best CD is this month? Wonder no more, I've got the answer.
>
> Whilst walking home from town last week with a smile ear to ear because i'd bought tickets to see Oasis in concert in July, I thought i'd pop into HMV to see if they had there new album in stock. Much to my delight they did, i couldn't wait to get home and put it on.
>
> When pressing play on my stereo I sat back to enjoy and boy did I enjoy. 11 tracks of pure Oasis, with some little numbers for the ladies and some all and out rock and roll for us music driven men.
>
> From start to finish it's amazing, with there new release 'Lyla' being number 3, there's a couple of arm wavers, to which I can't wait when I go to the concert and some classic Liam Gallagher tunes spread throughout the album. There's a mixture of everything chucked into one great album. For the reasonable sum of £11 or £14 for the special edition this is a steal.
>
> 'Can't believe the truth' is available at any good music store. Maybe some bad ones as well.

What did the examiner think?

Good features
- It sounds like a review.
- It is well organised with some interesting approaches, e.g. leaving the title of the CD until the end, linking the concert to the purchase of the CD, etc.
- There is a nice sense of audience.
- The reviewer's enthusiasm comes through.
- It is interesting.
- It is about the right length.
- It is mostly accurately written.

How it could be improved?
- A title?
- More care taken with spelling, e.g. 'there' instead of 'their'.
- Sorting out 'i' and 'I'.
- Taking more care with full stops.
- Getting rid of the clumsiness, e.g. 'to which I can't wait'.

Remember

A good review that contains basic errors will gain fewer marks than it deserves. Check your work carefully when you have finished writing.

Activity 20

Write a review of a music CD or downloaded album you have listened to recently. You will need to decide:
- who it is for
- where it is going to appear.

Remember that you can praise or criticise it, or a bit of both.

Book reviews

A book review gives a flavour of the book and will select parts of the book for more detailed comment. It will deal with what the book is about and how well it is written. In the case of fiction, it must not give too much away. Below is an example of a book review from a newspaper.

The Lighthouse

by P.D. James. Penguin £6.99

Set in an imaginary island off Cornwall, PD James' latest has all the ingredients that make her fiction so entertaining. Adam Dalgliesh may not be the sexiest fictional detective around, but he does have a winning way with a Shakespearean quote; and in this book his love life seems to have hotted up a bit, with a lovely young thing called Emma about to become the new Mrs D.

Fortunately, the romantic stuff doesn't get in the way of the real focus of the story, which, of course, is murder, and the investigation of it. Dalgliesh arrives on the remote island of Combe to find silence surrounding the murder he has been sent to solve. That the victim is a famous writer, whose body has been found hanging from the balcony of a lighthouse, gives the story an edge.

Adding to the tension – especially after another corpse is found – is the fact that this is a classic 'locked room' mystery, with no one able to reach or leave the island for the duration. As ever, the settings are effectively described and the police procedures convincing. All one has to do is sit back and enjoy the ride.

Activity 21

In pairs, list the features you can see in this real newspaper review of the novel *The Lighthouse*. Discuss how effective you think this review is. Would it make you want to read the book? If so, why?

Read the book review written by a student on page 163. Then look at the annotations and examiner comment.

'THE CURIOUS INCIDENT OF THE DOG IN THE NIGHT TIME' ❶

A story to ignite sympathy and understanding and plenty of laughs. ❷

Looking for a book that isn't BORING? Isn't TYPICAL? Is REFRESHING, ENLIGHTENING and FUNNY? ❸

Your search is over!

- I have read my way through heaps of books (do I sound sad?) and have met the tedious, the intellectual and the downright rubbish . . . until I opened Mark Haddon's 'The Curious Incident of the Dog in the Night time'. I have to admit I was stunned.

Why? What happens? ❹

- The book follows a journey of adventure, change and tragic reality, through the eyes of a boy with Asperger's Syndrome. Learn more and more about this syndrome and come to realise that people with this problem face huge difficulties in every day of their lives, yet they are just people.
- Haddon debunks that myth that kids with this syndrome are 'freaks' – read this and realise that they are to be envied for their bravery, and sometimes staggering mental ability.

So, it's good then?

- I suppose you could say the way it's written is a bit strange – unconventional, shall we say? The story is written with absolutely no description (because of the central character's illness), and this may be off-putting. However, despite its surface simplicity, it's still pretty cool and intellectual! (or so I like to kid myself!) ❺

Describe it in three words?

- SAD   • MOVING   • FUNNY ❻

Who is it suitable for?

- I'd say anyone who feels the need to understand the way other people work – in fact my friend who is just thirteen now wants to be a social worker after reading this novel. SO, there you are, early teens to adulthood, it's great for everyone!

YOUR FINAL PERSUASION . . .

❼ Read this book to change your perception of people. It will make you a better listener, and an excellent judge of character: one that looks beneath the surface of people before judging them, as the people learn to do in this novel, and as the central character himself does.

Go on – release your inner, open-minded book fiend and follow Christopher on his brave, brave journey . . .

You will not regret it.

(The Curious Incident . . . is available from all bookshops – £5.99 and great for pocket money!)

❶ It starts with the name of the book.

❷ It opens in a dynamic way.

❸ It goes on to capture the reader with three quick questions and the effective use of capitals.

❹ It gives a flavour of what the book is about.

❺ It expresses an opinion.

❻ Sub-headings and bullet points have been used cleverly.

❼ It ends with a recommendation.

Examiner tip

There are different ways of approaching the review task. Use a method you feel comfortable with, and which works.

Activity 22

Think of a book you have enjoyed reading. Write a review of it for your school magazine. Start by creating a plan based on what you have learnt so far in this section. Remember to:

- give the name of the book and its author
- give the price
- give a flavour of what the book is about
- say what you like and/or dislike about it
- give your recommendation.

Film reviews

A film review is likely to start with the name of the film. It may also name the director and/or main actors. It then gives an idea of what the film is about (without giving too much away), and ends with an opinion of its impact and the quality of the performances of those taking part. It will end with a recommendation that may take the form of a star rating.

On page 165 is a film review taken from a newspaper. The film is a documentary.

FILM REVIEWS

The Devil and Daniel Johnston

Among musical experts, Daniel Johnston is regarded as one of the great singer-songwriters of the last 20 years; his admirers have included David Bowie, Sonic Youth and the late Kurt Cobain. But in the mid-1980s, just when his career seemed to be taking off, he began to suffer from a mental illness from which he never recovered.

Jeff Feuerzeig's documentary uses interviews, home videos, archive footage and tapes to build a picture of his life. As an example of how to put a life on screen, it is exemplary in its thoroughness and willingness to allow a wide range of views. You see the beauty of his songs but also the dangerous madness.

Where it falls down is in the claim that Johnston is a lost genius. On the evidence of the music here, I'm intrigued but not convinced.

The Independent 5/5/06

This shows you what a review is intended to do. Some of its main features include:

- the heading, which tells you neatly what the review is about
- the first paragraph, which gives the context of the film and some interesting information
- the second paragraph, which gives you a flavour of how the film has been put together; it also includes some complimentary remarks
- the conclusion, which gives a brief but clear reaction.

Below is a student's review of the film *Pirates of the Caribbean*. Read it, then complete the activity that follows.

Pirates of the Caribbean

The Pirates of the Carabean is a stunning film on, guess what? . . . Pirates! Famous actors such as Jonny Depp and Orlando Bloom from Lord of the Rings star in this amazing film. The film contains high level of comedy and action.

This spectacular film is a masterpiece aimed at people in the ages of 6-16, However I really think it can be enjoyed by anybody with a sence of humour. If I was too rate this film it would be four stars out of five stars.

When this film was released it was in the top charts, this I think is due to the amount of comedy preformed by Johny Depp.

However Orlando bloom who plays Will Turner takes on a more serious role of the son of Bootstrap Bill.

The film shows a great storyline of Orlando Bloom being chased by scary ghost pirates, The pirates have sufferent from the curse of the black pearl. This is an epic adventure that is a MUST SEE! The special effects in this film is awesome. The ghost pirates look completely lifelike.

However the film lacks realism and is quite hard to believe, maybe for the ages of fourteen plus this film is quite unbelievable.

However I recommend this film to anybody with an imagination, I think that it can be enjoyed by all ages. I myself think that this film is great and a must see film. It is recommended not just by me but the Sun newspaper and the biggest video and dvd rental company 'blockbuster'. It is well worth the money you pay to see tis unique film.

Activity 23

1. For the film review on pages 165–166, decide which of the following statements you agree with, and say why.
   - The student has a good idea of what they are supposed to do.
   - A lot of the content is what you would expect in a film review.
   - It holds the reader's attention.
   - The tone is appropriate.
   - It is well organised.
   - It is accurately written.

2. Discuss and note down what you think the strengths and weaknesses of the review are. Include examples where possible.

What have I learnt?

In this section we covered:
- the different kinds of transactional writing: letters, reports, newspaper and magazine articles, leaflets, speeches and reviews
- the layout, tone and content in the different types of transactional writing
- types of Paper 2 Section B exam questions

How confident do you now feel about each of the above? You could note down the points you feel confident about and those you need to go back to.

Paper 1

Section A

*Read carefully the story below. Then answer **all** the questions that follow it on page 169.*

In the extract below, Harry Silver is a single parent who lives in London. His son, Pat, is four years old and has a bike called Bluebell. Cyd is an American woman who works as a waitress in a café. Harry and Pat have met her once before when they had breakfast in the café.

Pat liked to ride his bike by this open-air swimming pool at the edge of the park. […]

Long before the summer was over, the water would be drained from the pool and the odd supermarket trolley fished from the bottom. We were only in the middle of August, but the little pool had already been abandoned for another year by everyone apart from Pat and his Bluebell.

5 There was something depressing about the almost permanently empty pool. It was in a desolate part of the park, nowhere near the adventure playground where children screamed with delight, or the little café where mums and dads – but they were mostly mums – drank endless cups of tea. […] And to tell you the truth, it suited me to be away from all those mums.

I could see what they were thinking when we entered the park every morning.

10 Where's the mother?

Why isn't he at work? […]

'Daddy! Look at me!'

Pat was on the far side of the pool, breathing hard as he paused by the stubby little diving board that poked out over the empty deep end.

15 I smiled from the bench where I sat with my paper, and as soon as he saw that he had my attention he shot off again – eyes shining, hair flying, his little legs pumping furiously as he tore around the pool on Bluebell.

'Stay right away from the edge!'

'I will! I do!'

20 For the fifth time in five minutes, I read the opening sentence of an article about the collapse of the Japanese economy. […]

'Look at me now!'

The sight made me freeze.

Pat had very carefully edged his bike out on to the diving board. He was balanced above a ten-foot drop
25 to the pockmarked concrete at the bottom of the pool. Either side of Bluebell, his legs were at full stretch as he steadied himself with the toes of his dirty trainers. I hadn't seen him looking so happy for weeks.

'Stay right there,' I called. 'Don't move.'

His smile faded when he saw me start running towards him. I should have gone slower. I should have pretended that nothing was wrong. Because when he saw the look on my face, he started trying to back
30 off the diving board. But it was easier to get on than off and the world seemed to slip into slow motion as I saw one of Bluebell's stabilisers slide off the side of the diving board, spin in the air for a moment, and then Pat's little feet inside the dirty trainers were off balance and scrambling for something that wasn't there, and I was watching my boy and his bike falling headfirst into that empty swimming pool.

He was lying under the diving board, the bike on top of him, the blood starting to spread around his mop
35 of yellow hair. […]

'Oh Pat,' I said, pulling the bike off him and holding him far more tightly than I should have. 'Oh God,' I said, taking my mobile phone out of my jacket with fingers which were sticky from his blood, frantically tapping in the PIN number and hearing the beep-beep-beep sound of a flat battery.

I picked up my son.

40 I started to run.

You can't run far with a four-year-old child in your arms. They are already too big, too heavy, too awkward to carry with any speed.

I wanted to get Pat home to the car, but I staggered out of the park knowing that wasn't going to be quick enough.

45 I burst into the café where we had eaten green spaghetti, Pat still pale and silent and bleeding in my arms. It was lunch time, and the place was full of office workers in suits stuffing their faces. […]

'Get an ambulance!'

Nobody moved.

Then the kitchen doors flew open and Cyd came through them, a tray piled with food in one hand and
50 her order pad in the other. She looked at us for a moment, flinching at the sight of Pat's lifeless body, the blood all over my hands and shirt, the blind panic on my face.

Then she expertly slid the tray on to the nearest table and came towards us.

'It's my son! Get an ambulance!'

'It will be quicker if I drive you,' she said.

55 There were white lines on the hospital floor that directed you to the casualty department, but before we got anywhere near it we were surrounded by nurses and porters who took Pat from my arms and laid him on a trolley. It was a trolley for an adult, and he looked tiny on it. Just so tiny. […]

I tried to tell them about the bike on the diving board above the empty swimming pool, but I don't know if it made much sense to them. It didn't make much sense to me.

60 'We'll take care of him,' a nurse said, and the trolley banged through green swing doors. […]

Cyd gently took my arm.

'You have to let him go,' she said, and led me to a bleak little waiting area where she bought us coffee in polystyrene cups from a vending machine. […]

'Are you okay?' she said.

65 I shook my head. 'I'm so stupid.'

'These things happen. Do you know what happened to me when I was about that age?'

She waited for my reply. I looked up at her wide-set brown eyes.

'What?'

'I was watching some kids playing baseball and I went up and stood right behind the batter. Right behind
70 him.' She smiled at me. 'And when he swung back to hit the ball, he almost took my head off. That bat was only made of some kind of plastic, but it knocked me out cold. I actually saw stars. Look.'

She pushed the black veil of hair off her forehead. Just above her eyebrow there was a thin white scar about as long as a thumbnail.

'I know you feel terrible now,' she said. 'But kids are tough. They get through these things.'

75 'It was so high,' I said. 'And he fell so hard. The blood – it was everywhere.'

But I was grateful for Cyd's thin white scar. I appreciated the fact that she had been knocked unconscious as a child. It was good of her.

Question 1 Look at lines 1–21.
What impressions do you get of Harry Silver and his son in these lines?

You must refer to the text to support your answer. [10]

Question 2 Look at lines 22–48.
How does the writer convey tension and excitement in these lines? [10]

Question 3 Look at lines 49–77.
What are your thoughts and feelings about Cyd in these lines? [10]

Question 4 Now consider the whole passage.
Imagine you are Cyd. Write your diary entry for the day when Harry Silver arrived in the café with his injured son. [10]

Section B

*Answer Question B1 **and** Question B2.*

B1. Imagine you are in a queue in a post office or a shop. Describe what you see and hear as you wait to be served. [20]

B2. Choose **one** of the following titles for your writing. [20]

a. The rebel

b. Write about a time when you were treated unfairly.

c. Continue the following: 'I had been looking forward to a relaxing evening …'

d. Write about an occasion when you had a narrow escape.

e. Coming home

Paper 2

Section A

Answer **all** *the following questions.*

Look at the extracts from a booklet on waste and recycling, produced by Friends of the Earth (pages 171–173).

Question 1
List five problems caused by current ways of disposing of waste. [5]

Question 2
List **five** ways that we can reduce waste when we buy food and clothes. [5]

Question 3
How do the extracts from the Friends of the Earth booklet try to persuade you to reduce waste?

You should consider:
- the arguments used in the extract
- the persuasive techniques used. [10]

Now look at the newspaper article, 'Recycling can be a complete waste (of time)' (page 174).

Question 4
According to the article, why is recycling a waste of time and what should be our priorities? [10]

For this next question, you will need to consider both texts.

Question 5
Both of these texts are about recycling waste and saving resources.

Compare the two texts under the following headings:

- The information each text gives about recycling in Britain compared with other countries
- The way other facts and figures are used in each text
- The use of photographs and illustrations in each text. [10]

Wasted times

Most of the things that we throw away could be a valuable resource for someone, somewhere. That's why when we call something "waste" we are making a mistake. The problem is that we are a nation addicted to chucking stuff out.

Stuff that we no longer want ends up buried in landfill or burnt in incinerators. These disposal methods pollute our land, water and air. Landfill sites can cause health problems in local communities, pollute our water supplies and release methane (adding to dangerous climate change). And incinerators produce toxic air pollution as well as toxic ash, which then has nowhere to go but into landfill. Our rubbish is piling up problems for the environment and for the future.

Our endless appetite for new things is adding to these problems. For every tonne of new products we buy, 10 tonnes of resources are used to manufacture them, as well as huge amounts of energy. This energy comes from burning fossil fuels such as coal, oil and gas, which release carbon dioxide. The rising level of carbon dioxide in the atmosphere is the main cause of climate change, the single biggest environmental threat facing the planet.

That's why Friends of the Earth is campaigning for more of our rubbish to be recycled, not incinerated or buried in landfill. Why send our rubbish up in smoke when we could recycle it into something useful?

We don't have to waste our waste. This booklet explains how we can reduce our waste, and how recycling can help the environment, save resources and energy and generate jobs.

Did you know

The average person in the UK throws out their body weight in rubbish every three months.

In 2002 research suggested that babies born within three kilometres of landfill sites taking hazardous waste are 40 per cent more likely to have genetic conditions like Down's Syndrome.

PhotoDisc

2

What's in your bin?

Paper
The day-to-day demand for paper is putting immense pressure on the world's forests. Instead of using paper once and throwing it away, we can recycle it to make more paper and cardboard.

Kitchen and garden waste
What a waste to throw our green waste away. Peat bogs are rare and valuable wildlife habitats, and they're being destroyed to make cheap garden compost when we could make it at home for free.

25%

35%

11%

9%

9%

11%

Plastic
Most plastic is made almost entirely from oil. When we throw plastic away it takes hundreds of years to degrade in landfill and produces toxic smoke if burnt in incinerators. But we could cut our plastic use by refusing plastic bags and over-packaged items.

Glass
Our glass recycling rate is one of the lowest in Europe. But 30 gallons of oil are saved for every tonne of glass which is recycled.

The rest
Old clothes and shoes, electrical items, toys and the rest of our rubbish. Even some of these items could be passed on to others, given to clothes banks or recycled in other ways.

Metals
Two-thirds of the metal in our bins comes from steel or aluminium cans and foil. All of these can be easily and profitably recycled, with massive savings in resources and energy.

Reduce, Re-use, Recycle

We can all reduce the amount we throw away. Here's how:

Reduce
Only buy products you really need which are durable and repairable. Don't accept excess packaging and refuse plastic bags. Buy fresh fruit and vegetables loose rather than ready-made meals. Make use of libraries, tool-hire shops, launderettes, nappy-washing services and car-hire companies whenever you can, rather than buying new products.

Re-use
Repair broken items such as clothes, shoes, electronic items and furniture. Buy from salvage yards and second-hand shops as much as you can. Give usable clothes, shoes and toys to charity shops. Ask suppliers if they will take back items to use again (like clothes hangers). Buy food, drinks and toiletries in returnable containers, and ask local shops to stock them. Ask your school or workplace to provide re-usable cups, plates, cutlery and hand-towels.

Recycle
Do your best to recycle as much of your waste as possible, at home, school or work. Try to buy products which are made from recycled materials. Compost as much as you can. Contact your council if they do not provide adequate recycling facilities, or set up a community scheme. Doorstep collection schemes are the most effective ways to collect waste. We take more personal responsibility for our waste if we separate it at home.

By reducing the amount we throw away, re-using everything we can, recycling and composting we can start to solve the waste crisis.

Did you know

Friends of the Earth studies have shown that 80 per cent of our waste could be recycled or composted.

Switzerland and the Netherlands already recycle half their waste. Our average in the UK is only about 11 per cent.

Daventry District Council in Northamptonshire achieved recycling rates of 53 per cent in 2000-2001.

Martin Jenkinson/Alamy

If we could recycle 30 per cent of our waste by 2005 we could create 45,000 green jobs.

8

Recycling can be a complete waste (of time)

MILLIONS of Britons may be wasting their time by recycling, experts said yesterday.

Consumers are led to believe that recycling materials and choosing certain types of packaging is of significant benefit to the environment.

But they are minor considerations compared to what car we drive and how much energy we use to heat our homes, according to a report.

Driving to the bottle bank to recycle a few empty wine and beer bottles typically uses more energy than it saves due to petrol consumption, the author warns.

'If you are going to the bottle bank you should always combine it with another trip,' said environmental consultant Dr Jan. Kooijman. 'Otherwise it becomes completely pointless and can actually waste more energy than it saves.'

He says changing from a four-wheel drive vehicle which manages only 20mpg to a typical

By **Robin Yapp**
Science Reporter

family saloon car that does 40mpg can save 264 gallons of fuel in a year.

Yet it would take 40 years of recycling all the family's glass bottles to save the same amount, he adds.

Dr Kooijman, a Dutch former physics professor, says the average British household uses about 250 gigajoules (JGs) of energy a year.

A gigajoule is a standard energy measurement. On heating and hot water, for example, the average home burns 50–100 GJs annually.

Putting on a sweater and lowering the temperature at home by 2°C could save six GJs a year – almost as much as the total energy required to producing all the packaging a family goes through in the same time.

The findings suggest that the declining marriage rate and the breakdown of the 'nuclear family' are closely related to

the increased level of waste, because people living alone produce about twice as much rubbish.

The report was commissioned by the Industry Council for Packaging and the Environment (INCPEN), which represents 60 major companies including Sainsbury's, McDonald's and Boots.

Director Jane Bickerstaffe said: 'People worry about whether they should use disposable nappies or non-disposable ones when environmentally there is no difference.

'Consumers should choose what best suits their needs and not feel guilty about trivial decisions.'

A Mori poll showed that nearly half the people in Britain take part in recycling schemes, but far fewer consider it important to cut down on car journeys (11 per cent) and electricity (eight per cent).

Theresa May, Conservative spokesman for transport and the environment, said: 'The

Driving down to the bottle bank can cause more harm than good

Government is failing all round in this area. It's failing to meet its recycling targets, with rates lower than in much of Europe.

'But it is also failing to provide public transport that people feel is reliable. In many areas they are forcing people off public transport and back into their cars.'

A spokesman for the Department of Transport said: 'We are investing

£33billion over the next ten years for the railways, light rail use has grown by 86 per cent over the past six years and we have halted the long-term decline in bus use with a two per cent increase last year.'

The Department for Environment, Food and Rural Affairs added: 'Very few people would argue that it's Government's job to tell people what car to drive.'

Section B

Answer Question B1 **and** *Question B2.*

B1. You are a member of your school or college Student Council. Your headteacher has asked the Council to suggest ways in which the school can reduce waste and become more actively involved in re-cycling. You have been asked to write a report, giving the Student Council's views to the Governing Body of the school.

Write your report. [20]

B2. A magazine is running a series of articles reviewing the year's best releases in:
- film
- music.

The articles are aimed at teenagers.

Choose one of these topics and write your review of the year's best film or music album. [20]